ELEVEN SHORT PLAYS

for drama students & amateur theatre

Also by Martin Foreman

Novels
Weekend
The Butterfly's Wing

Short Stories
A Sense of Loss
First and Fiftieth

Plays
Angel
Californian Lives
Casanova Dreaming
Now We Are Pope
Tadzio Speaks (*aka* Death on the Lido)
The Satyricon
Ben Jonson's Volpone

Non-Fiction
AIDS and Men (ed)

martinforeman.com

ELEVEN SHORT PLAYS

for drama students & amateur theatre

Martin Foreman

Arbery Books

arberybooks.co.uk

August 2023

Published by Arbery Books
17/5 Craigend Park, Edinburgh EH16 5XX
printed by copyshop.co.uk, Redditch B98 8LG

ISBN: 978-0-9933546-7-0

The Plays

* *In other plays there are comic moments but the comedy is incidental to the plot.*

Notes

With one exception (*The Report)* these plays were inspired by 28 Plays Later from The Literal Challenge in 2023. I offer my thanks for the impetus and I forward to repeating the challenge in future years.

Performing rights:

For use in drama courses and acting workshops: no charge
For public performances where the audience does not pay for any part of the programme: no charge
For a paying audience: from £10 per performance.

In all cases, including drama courses and acting workshops, rights must be obtained in advance.

For further information and to apply for rights, contact the author at martin@martinforeman.com.

AGAIN AND AGAIN
ONE MORE TIME

CAST
ABBEY   BURNS   CORNELL

ABBEY at a complicated console muttering as they frantically consult monitors, click switches and connect and undo connections. A loud hum from the console dies down as ABBEY's actions settle into a routine.

ABBEY   A off, G3 on, check screen left, A on, disconnect lower plug, G3 off, reconnect lower plug, stand back. One more time. A off, G3 on, check screen left, A on, disconnect lower plug, G3 off, reconnect lower plug, stand back. One more time.

Enter BURNS and CORNELL

ABBEY   *(continuing the routine)* Thank Heavens.

BURNS   Anything wrong?

ABBEY   No, no, no. I just need a bathroom break, that's all.

BURNS   This is Cornell, (s)he's going to take over.

ABBEY   One second. Check screen. Wel... Disconnect ...come.

CORNELL   Hi.

BURNS   It's very simple.

CORNELL   It looks complicated.

BURNS   No, no, no, not in the least, is it, Abbey?

ABBEY   Of course not. It's simply a matter of . . . G3 on . . . and making sure that . . . Check screen left. You'll soon get used to it.

CORNELL   What exactly does it do?

BURNS   Ah . . . Can you explain, Abbey?

1

ABBEY   Basically, it monitors the input, records, calibrates and
             adjusts as necessary. Then it converts to the output,
             which varies, of course, according to demand, which
             you can see here . . . No, sorry, not there, that's the
             equaliser – it's on the blink but that doesn't matter as
             long as . . . Excuse me. *(adjusts something)*

BURNS   Well, I'll leave you both to get on with it. You don't
             want me hanging around, peering over your shoulder
             making you nervous.

CORNELL   I'm a bit nervous already.

BURNS   Don't be, don't be. There's nothing to be nervous
             about as long as you follow the routine, right, Abbey?

ABBEY   What? No, it's very simple, very easy. I'll soon show
             you how.

CORNELL   So, I'm taking over from you.

ABBEY   Yes and no. You're taking over from the last operator –
             what was their name?

BURNS   It's on the tip of my tongue, no, it's gone. Nice chap, or
             was it a woman? I don't remember. Some people don't
             stay very long.

CORNELL   What happened to them?

BURNS   Moved on.

ABBEY   I'm just filling in temporarily. My work is quite
             different. I don't usually do this. But you'll be fine.

CORNELL   What do you do?

ABBEY   There's a question. You need to be here a little longer
             before I answer that. You see, everyone's work
             depends on someone else. There's throughput and
             you wouldn't understand what I do before you have a
             thorough grasp of what you do and what everyone

else in the building . . .

BURNS   Not just this building.

ABBEY   True, true. What also goes on in X12, the port facility and at the air hub. Once you've grasped that you've grasped everything and you won't need to ask what I do.

BURNS   Just as people don't need to ask what you do because they have a holistic view of the whole operation.

CORNELL   And what is it I do?

ABBEY   Stand here – that's right. Now watch me, read the instructions on that sheet and keep your eye on the monitor. It's very simple.

CORNELL   I'm not sure.

ABBEY   Very easy. Look. First, A off, then G3 on, check screen left, A on, disconnect lower plug, G3 off, reconnect lower plug, stand back.

CORNELL   A off, screen on, G off, lower plug . . .

ABBEY   No, A off, G3 on, check screen left, A on, disconnect lower plug, G3 off, reconnect lower plug, stand back.

CORNELL   What am I checking on the screen?

ABBEY   You'll see. Ah, it's defaulted. So we need to reverse the procedure. G3 on, connect lower plug, A off, screen right, G3 off, A on. Got it?

BURNS   You'll be fine. I'll be back in an hour to check everything's going smoothly. Until then you're in capable hands.

Exit BURNS

ABBEY   A off, G3 on, check screen left, A on, disconnect lower plug, G3 off, reconnect lower plug, stand back . . .

CORNELL   Can I just ask . . .

ABBEY   Pay attention. A off . . . Ah, so that's happened, we need to reset. Everything off except B4 and start again. Can't take too long, however, or the system input will back up and the shit will really hit the fan. That's not a metaphor, by the way, just collateral damage. Right, are you ready? No point in me carrying on. You just take over. I'll guide you. So, A off, G3 on, check screen left . . .

CORNELL   What am I checking?

ABBEY   A on, disconnect lower plug. G3 off, stand back. Repeat after me, A off.

CORNELL   A off.

ABBEY   G3 on.

CORNELL   G3 on.

ABBEY   Check screen left.

CORNELL   Check screen – what for?

ABBEY   A on.

CORNELL   A on.

ABBEY   Disconnect lower plug.

CORNELL   It's already disconnected.

ABBEY   That saves time. G3 off.

CORNELL   G3 off.

ABBEY   Reconnect lower plug.

CORNELL is confused

ABBEY   Reconnect lower plug.

CORNELL   Reconnect lower plug.

ABBEY   Stand back.

4

CORNELL   Stand back. Couldn't a computer do all this?

ABBEY   Again. A off.

CORNELL   A off.

ABBEY   Probably. G3 on.

CORNELL   So why not? G3 on.

ABBEY   Good question. Check screen. Left screen!

CORNELL   I still don't know what for.

ABBEY   Connect lower plug.

CORNELL   You said disconnect!

ABBEY   Depends on the screen. G3 off.

CORNELL   G3 off.

ABBEY   A on.

CORNELL   A on.

ABBEY   Stand back.

CORNELL   Stand back. So why not a computer?

ABBEY   Ask me in the break. Together . . .

They repeat the complete mantra together,

ABBEY & CORNELL

A off, G3 on, check screen left, A on, disconnect lower plug, G3 off, reconnect lower plug, stand back. One more time. A off, G3 on, check screen left, A on, disconnect lower plug, G3 off, reconnect lower plug, stand back. One more time.

A off, G3 on, check screen left, A on, disconnect lower plug, G3 off, reconnect lower plug, stand back. One more time. A off, G3 on, check screen left, A on,

Eleven Short Plays

A & C (cont)   disconnect lower plug, G3 off, reconnect lower plug, stand back. One more time.

A off, G3 on, check screen left, A on, disconnect lower plug, G3 off, reconnect lower plug, stand back. One more time. A off, G3 on, check screen left, A on, disconnect lower plug, G3 off, reconnect lower plug, stand back. One more time.

ABBEY   You've got it. Show me.

CORNELL   A off, G3 on, check screen left, A on, disconnect lower plug, G3 off, reconnect lower plug, stand back.

ABBEY   Getting there. Need to be faster. One more time.

CORNELL   A off, G3 on, check screen left, A on, disconnect lower plug, G3 off, , reconnect lower plug, stand back.

ABBEY   One more time

CORNELL   A off, G3 on, check screen left, A on, disconnect lower plug, G3 off, reconnect lower plug, stand back.

ABBEY   Perfect. I'll leave you. Been dying for a piss.

Exit ABBEY

CORNELL   A off, G3 on, check screen left, A on, disconnect lower plug, G3 off, reconnect lower plug, stand back. One more time. A off, G3 on, check screen left, A on, disconnect lower plug, G3 off, reconnect lower plug, stand back. One more time. A off, G3 on, check screen left, A on, disconnect lower plug, G3 off, reconnect lower plug, stand back. One more time.

Enter ABBEY

ABBEY   *(while CORNELL repeats the mantra)* You've got it.

ABBEY sits back, munches a sandwich and checks their phone while CORNELL repeats the mantra faster and faster. As they do so, the console hum becomes louder and louder until

CORNELL   Disconnect . . . reconnect . . . disconnect lower plug?

There is a flash from the console, electrocuting CORNELL, who collapses. A siren goes off. ABBEY drops everything, rushes to CORNELL as BURNS rushes in.

ABBEY   It's happened again!

BURNS   Get him/her out of here, I'll take over.

ABBEY drags CORNELL off as BURNS switches off the siren, frantically consults monitors, clicks switches, connects and undoes connections. The hum from the console dies down as their actions settle into a routine and their words become clearer.

BURNS   A off, G3 on, check screen left, A on, disconnect lower plug, G3 off, reconnect lower plug, stand back. One more time. A off, G3 on, check screen left, A on, disconnect lower plug, G3 off, reconnect lower plug, stand back. One more time.

Enter ABBEY and CORNELL

BURNS   *(continuing the routine)* Thank Heavens.

CORNELL   Anything wrong?

BURNS   No, no, no. I just need a bathroom break, that's all.

CORNELL   This is Abbey, (s)he's going to take over.

BURNS   One second. Check screen Wel... Disconnect ...come.

ABBEY   Hi

CORNELL   Now, it's very simple.

ABBEY   It looks complicated.

CORNELL   No, no, no, not in the least, is it, Burns?

BURNS   Of course not. It's simply a matter of . . . G3 on . . . and making sure that . . . Check screen left. You'll soon get used to it.

ABBEY   What exactly does it do?

CORNELL   Ah . . . Can you explain, Burns?

BURNS   Basically, it monitors the input, records, calibrates and adjusts as necessary. Then it is converted into the output, which varies, of course, according to demand, which you can see here . . . No, sorry, not there, that's the equaliser – it's on the blink but that doesn't matter as long as . . . Excuse me *(adjusts something)*

CORNELL   Well, I'll leave you both to get on with it. You don't want me hanging around, peering over your shoulder making you nervous.

ABBEY   I'm a bit nervous already.

CORNELL   Don't be, don't be. There's nothing to be nervous about as long as you follow the routine, right, Burns?

BURNS   What? No, it's very simple, very easy. I'll soon show you how.

ABBEY   So, I'm taking over from you.

BURNS   Yes and no. You're taking over from the last operator – what was their name?

CORNELL   It's on the tip of my tongue, no, it's gone. Nice chap, or was it a woman? I don't remember. Some people don't stay very long.

ABBEY   What happened to them?

CORNELL   Moved on.

BURNS   I'm just filling in temporarily. My usual work is quite different. I don't usually do this. But you'll be fine – just follow the instructions there.

ABBEY   What do you do?

BURNS   There's a question. You need to be here a little longer before I answer that. You see, everyone's work depends on someone else. There's throughput and you wouldn't understand what I do before you have a

thorough grasp of what you do and what everyone
else in the building . . .

CORNELL   Not just this building.

BURNS   True, true. What also goes on in X12, the port facility
             and at the air hub. Once you've grasped that you've
             grasped everything and you won't need to ask what I
             do?

CORNELL   Just as people don't need to ask what you do because
             they have a holistic view of the whole operation.

ABBEY   And what is it I do?

BURNS   Stand here – that's right. Now watch me, read the
             instructions on that sheet and keep your eye on the
             monitor. It's very simple.

ABBEY   I'm not sure.

BURNS   Very easy. Look. First, A off, then G3 on, check screen
             left, A on, disconnect lower plug, G3 off, reconnect
             lower plug, stand back.

ABBEY   A off, screen on, G off, lower plug

BURNS   No, A off, G3 on, check screen left, A on, disconnect
             lower plug, G3 off, reconnect lower plug, stand back.

ABBEY   What am I checking on the screen?

BURNS   You'll see. Ah, it's defaulted. So we need to reverse the
             procedure. G3 on, connect lower plug, A off, screen
             right, G3 off, A on. Got it?

CORNELL   You'll be fine. I'll be back in an hour to check
             everything's going smoothly. Until then you're in
             capable hands.

Exit CORNELL

BURNS   A off, G3 on, check screen left, A on, disconnect lower
             plug, G3 off, reconnect lower plug, stand back . . .

ABBEY	Can I just ask . . .
BURNS	Pay attention. A off . . . Ah, so that's happened, we need to reset. Everything off except B4 and start again. Can't take too long, however, or the system input will back up and the shit will really hit the fan. That's not a metaphor, by the way, just collateral damage. Right, are you ready? No point in me carrying on. You just take over. I'll guide you. So, A off, G3 on, check screen left . . .
ABBEY	What am I checking?
BURNS	A on, disconnect lower plug. G3 off, stand back. Repeat after me, A off.
ABBEY	A off
BURNS	G3 on
ABBEY	G3 on
BURNS	check screen left
ABBEY	check screen – what for?
BURNS	A on.
ABBEY	A on.
BURNS	Disconnect lower plug
ABBEY	It's already disconnected.
BURNS	That saves time. G3 off
ABBEY	G3 off.
BURNS	Reconnect lower plug.

ABBEY is confused.

BURNS	Reconnect lower plug.
ABBEY	Reconnect lower plug.
BURNS	Stand back

ABBEY   Stand back. Couldn't a computer do all this?

BURNS   Again. A off

ABBEY   A off

BURNS   Probably. G3 on

ABBEY   So why not? G3 on.

BURNS   Good question. Check screen. Left screen!

ABBEY   I still don't know what for.

BURNS   Connect lower plug.

ABBEY   You said disconnect!

BURNS   Depends on the screen. G3 off.

ABBEY   G3 off.

BURNS   A on.

ABBEY   A on.

BURNS   Stand back.

ABBEY   Stand back. So why not a computer?

BURNS   Ask me in the break. Together . . .

They repeat the complete mantra together

BURNS & ABBEY

            A off, G3 on, check screen left, A on, disconnect lower
            plug, G3 off, reconnect lower plug, stand back. One
            more time. A off, G3 on, check screen left, A on,
            disconnect lower plug, G3 off, reconnect lower plug,
            stand back. One more time.

            A off, G3 on, check screen left, A on, disconnect lower
            plug, G3 off, reconnect lower plug, stand back. One
            more time. A off, G3 on, check screen left, A on,
            disconnect lower plug, G3 off, reconnect lower plug,
            stand back. One more time.

B & A (cont)   A off, G3 on, check screen left, A on, disconnect lower plug, G3 off, reconnect lower plug, stand back. One more time. A off, G3 on, check screen left, A on, disconnect lower plug, G3 off, reconnect lower plug, stand back. One more time.

BURNS   You've got it. Show me.

ABBEY   A off, G3 on, check screen left, A on, disconnect lower plug, G3 off, reconnect lower plug, stand back.

BURNS   Getting there. Need to be faster. One more time.

ABBEY   A off, G3 on, check screen left, A on, disconnect lower plug, G3 off, reconnect lower plug, stand back.

BURNS   One more time

ABBEY   A off, G3 on, check screen left, A on, disconnect lower plug, G3 off, reconnect lower plug, stand back.

BURNS   Perfect. I'll leave you. Been dying for a piss.

Exit BURNS

ABBEY   A off, G3 on, check screen left, A on, disconnect lower plug, G3 off, reconnect lower plug, stand back. One more time. A off, G3 on, check screen left, A on, disconnect lower plug, G3 off, reconnect lower plug, stand back. One more time. A off, G3 on, check screen left, A on, disconnect lower plug, G3 off, reconnect lower plug, stand back. One more time.

Enter BURNS

BURNS *(while ABBEY repeats the mantra)* You've got it.

BURNS sits back, munches a sandwich and checks their phone while ABBEY repeats the mantra faster and faster. As they do so, the console hum becomes louder and louder until

ABBEY   Disconnect . . . connect . . . disconnect lower plug?

There is a flash from the console, electrocuting ABBEY, who collapses. A siren goes off. BURNS drops everything, rushes to ABBEY as CORNELL rushes in.

BURNS   It's happened again!

CORNELL   Get him/her out of here, I'll take over.

BURNS drags ABBEY off as CORNELL switches off the siren, frantically consults monitors, clicks switches, connects and undoes connections. The hum from the console dies down as their actions settle into a routine and their words become clearer.

CORNELL   A off, G3 on, check screen left, A on, disconnect lower plug, G3 off, reconnect lower plug, stand back. One more time. A off, G3 on, check screen left, A on, disconnect lower plug, G3 off, reconnect lower plug, stand back. One more time.

AGAIN AND AGAIN

THE REPORT

(winner: Pitlochry Festival Theatre Short Play Award, 2018)

CAST

EVANS   MCDONALD   THOMSON

A modern office; at least one file on the desk.

THOMSON by the window and McDONALD by the door

THOMSON   Bring Evans in.

McDONALD exits. THOMSON sits in the manager's chair and looks through the file on the desk. EVANS enters with McDONALD

THOMSON   Take a seat.

EVANS sits; McDONALD stands by the door

THOMSON   You've seen the report?

EVANS   Yes.

THOMSON   You've seen your name.

EVANS   Yes.

THOMSON   In several places.

EVANS   Yes.

THOMSON   Do you have any comment?

EVANS   It was dreadful. More than dreadful. Appalling. Heartbreaking.

THOMSON   That's all?

EVANS   What more can I say?

THOMSON   Do you not accept responsibility?

EVANS   Responsibility?

THOMSON   Yes.

EVANS	Why should I?
THOMSON	You were the architect.
EVANS	One of the architects.
THOMSON	The lead architect.
EVANS	It was a collegial effort.
THOMSON	Your name came first.
EVANS	Yes.
THOMSON	It was your signature.
EVANS	Yes.
THOMSON	Your responsibility.
EVANS	The studio's.
THOMSON	Ultimately yours. You signed.
EVANS	We followed standard procedures. We met all the legal regulations.
THOMSON	They failed.
EVANS	That wasn't my fault.
THOMSON	You signed.
EVANS	Yes.
THOMSON	People died.
EVANS	I know.
THOMSON	In pain.
EVANS	I know.
THOMSON	In agony.
EVANS	I know.
THOMSON	In a blazing inferno.
EVANS	I was there. I heard the screams.

THOMSON	If not you, who was responsible ?
EVANS	Construction is complicated. Many organisations, hundreds of people, had input. We followed guidelines. If there was a problem, it should have been identified. We did our bit. Someone else should have drawn attention to it.
THOMSON	Their failure doesn't absolve you of responsibility.
EVANS	Responsibility should be shared.
THOMSON	Then accept your share. Your colleagues. Your studio. You. People died.
EVANS	Do you think I don't know? I told you, I heard the screams. People screaming. Screaming, screaming, screaming.
THOMSON	What happens now?
EVANS	I don't know. I can't think.
THOMSON	You cannot do nothing.
EVANS	What? I can't think.
THOMSON	A response is needed.
EVANS	I can't think. *(coughs)* I feel ill.
THOMSON	People died.
EVANS	I know, I know! *(a paroxysm of coughing)* I can't breathe.

EVANS falls forward on to the desk. McDONALD rushes forward.

THOMSON	Get a glass of water.

McDONALD exits. THOMSON comes round the desk and pulls EVANS upright. EVANS begins to recover.

THOMSON	Are you all right?
EVANS	Yes.

THOMSON   Are you sure?

EVANS stands up

EVANS   I just need some air.

THOMSON   Open the window.

EVANS walks to the window, visibly recovering. Instead of opening the window:

EVANS   Bring McDonald in.

THOMSON exits. EVANS sits in the manager's chair and looks through the file on the desk. McDONALD enters with THOMSON

EVANS   Take a seat.

McDONALD sits. THOMSON stands by the door.

EVANS   You've seen the report?

McDONALD   Yes.

EVANS   You've seen your name.

McDONALD   Yes.

EVANS   In several places.

McDONALD   Yes.

EVANS   Do you have any comment?

McDONALD   It was dreadful. More than dreadful. Appalling. Heartbreaking.

EVANS   That's all?

McDONALD   What more can I say?

EVANS   Do you not accept responsibility?

McDONALD   Responsibility?

EVANS   Yes.

McDONALD   Why should I?

EVANS	You were on the committee.
McDONALD	So were others.
EVANS	You were chair of the committee.
McDONALD	It was voted on.
EVANS	As chair you cast the decisive vote.
McDONALD	Yes.
EVANS	It was your signature.
McDONALD	Yes.
EVANS	Your responsibility.
McDONALD	The Council's.
EVANS	Ultimately yours. You signed.
McDONALD	We followed standard procedures. We met all the legal regulations.
EVANS	They failed.
McDONALD	That wasn't my fault.
EVANS	You signed.
McDONALD	Yes.
EVANS	People died.
McDONALD	I know.
EVANS	In pain.
McDONALD	I know.
EVANS	In agony.
McDONALD	I know.
EVANS	In a blazing inferno.
McDONALD	I was there. I saw the flames.
EVANS	If not you, who was responsible ?

McDONALD	Construction is complicated. Many organisations, hundreds of people, had input. We followed guidelines. If there was a problem, it should have been identified. We did our bit. Someone else should have drawn attention to it.
EVANS	Their failure doesn't absolve you of responsibility.
McDONALD	Responsibility should be shared.
EVANS	Then accept your share. Your committee. The council. You. People died.
McDONALD	Do you think I don't know? I told you, I saw the flames. Flames everywhere. Burning. Everywhere burning, burning, burning.
EVANS	What happens now?
McDONALD	I don't know. I can't think.
EVANS	You cannot do nothing.
McDONALD	What? I can't think.
EVANS	A response is needed.
McDONALD	I can't think. *(coughs)* I feel ill.
EVANS	People died.
McDONALD	I know, I know! *(a paroxysm of coughing)* I can't breathe.

McDONALD falls forward on to the desk. THOMSON rushes forward.

EVANS	Get a glass of water.

THOMSON exits. EVANS comes round the desk and pulls McDONALD upright. McDONALD begins to recover.

EVANS	Are you all right?
McDONALD	Yes.
EVANS	Are you sure?

McDONALD stands up

McDONALD   I just need some air.

EVANS   Open the window.

McDONALD walks to the window, visibly recovering. Instead of opening the window:

McDONALD   Bring Thomson in.

EVANS exits. McDONALD sits in the manager's chair and looks through the file on the desk. THOMSON enters with EVANS

McDONALD   Take a seat.

THOMSON sits. EVANS stands by the door.

McDONALD   You've seen the report?

THOMSON   Yes.

McDONALD   You've seen your name.

THOMSON   Yes.

McDONALD   In several places.

THOMSON   Yes.

McDONALD   Do you have any comment?

THOMSON   It was dreadful. More than dreadful. Appalling. Heartbreaking.

McDONALD   That's all?

THOMSON   What more can I say?

McDONALD   Do you not accept responsibility?

THOMSON   Responsibility?

McDONALD   Yes.

THOMSON   Why should I?

McDONALD   You undertook the safety checks.

THOMSON   We worked as a team.

McDONALD   You led the team.

THOMSON   We followed guidelines.

McDONALD   You were team leader.

THOMSON   Yes.

McDONALD   It was your signature.

THOMSON   Yes.

McDONALD   Your responsibility.

THOMSON   The company's.

McDONALD   Ultimately yours. You signed.

THOMSON   We followed standard procedures. We met all
                 the legal regulations.

McDONALD   They failed.

THOMSON   That wasn't my fault.

McDONALD   You signed.

THOMSON   Yes.

McDONALD   People died.

THOMSON   I know.

McDONALD   In pain.

THOMSON   I know.

McDONALD   In agony.

THOMSON   I know.

THOMSON   I was there. I saw the smoke.

McDONALD   If not you, who was responsible ?

THOMSON   Construction is complicated. Many organisations,
                 hundreds of people, had input. We followed

	guidelines. If there was a problem, it should have been identified. We did our bit. Someone else should have drawn attention to it .
McDONALD	That doesn't absolve you of responsibility.
THOMSON	Responsibility should be shared.
McDONALD	Then accept your share. Your team. Your company. You. People died.
THOMSON	Do you think I don't know? I told you, I saw the smoke. Like a cloud, a volcano. Everywhere thick, thick smoke.
McDONALD	What happens now?
THOMSON	I don't know. I can't think.
McDONALD	You cannot do nothing.
THOMSON	What? I can't think.
McDONALD	A response is needed.
THOMSON	I can't think. *(coughs)* I feel ill.
McDONALD	People died.
THOMSON	I know, I know! *(a paroxysm of coughing)* I can't breathe.

THOMSON falls forward on to the desk. EVANS rushes forward.

McDONALD	Get a glass of water.

McDONALD comes round the desk to pull THOMSON upright, while EVANS goes to the door, opens and slams it shut again.

EVANS	My God.
McDONALD	What?
EVANS	*(coughs)* The building's on fire.

The scene quickly degenerates into coughing and fear.

McDONALD	Is it serious?

EVANS	It's everywhere. We can't get out.
McDONALD	The window.
THOMSON	What's happening?
McDONALD	There's a fire.
EVANS	It won't open.
McDONALD	Are you sure?
THOMSON	Try again.
EVANS	It won't move.
McDONALD	Break it!
THOMSON	No, the smoke outside. It'll come in.
McDONALD	What can we do?
EVANS	The advice is to wait.

The stage darkens as the fire takes over. The coughing continues.

THOMSON	The building is safe.
EVANS	The fire will be contained. It's designed that way.
THOMSON	The materials are fireproof.
McDONALD	Passed all the safety checks.
EVANS	At every stage of construction.
THOMSON	It's safe.
EVANS	We'll be safe.
McDONALD	Safe.
THOMSON	Safe.
EVANS	Safe.

The voices diminish as the blackout becomes complete. Screams are heard.

Light comes up on the scene at the beginning:

THOMSON   Bring Evans in.

McDONALD exits. THOMSON takes the manager's seat and looks through the file on the desk.

COMEDY

DELIVERY!

CAST

ANDREW (40s)   KATE (40s)   CHARLIE (18)   COURIER (20+)
Charlie and Courier can be M or F or N
The Courier works for different companies (A), (B), (C)
but is always the same person and personality

Open plan; front door to one side of the stage; door to the rest of the house opposite.

Doorbell: ANDREW enters

ANDREW   I'll get it.

ANDREW opens door to COURIER (A)

COURIER   Jackson?

ANDREW   Yes.

COURIER   Delivery. *(hands ANDREW a package)* Stand back.

COURIER takes photo of ANDREW with the package

COURIER   Proof of receipt. Thanks. Bye.

COURIER exits

ANDREW   Goodbye.

CHARLIE enters, eyes on phone

CHARLIE   I was expecting that.

ANDREW   It's for your mother.

KATE enters

KATE   That my samples?

ANDREW   No idea. Want coffee?

KATE   No time. *(opens package)* Damn!

ANDREW	What?
KATE	The new range is supposed to be midnight, dark ebony, light charcoal and sable. They've sent midnight, sable, light ebony and dark charcoal.
ANDREW	Send them back.
CHARLIE	*(checking phone)* Yes!!!
KATE	*(on phone)* Pick-up. Return item.
CHARLIE	I've just hit ten thousand!
ANDREW	Congratulations. Ten thousand what?
CHARLIE	Followers.
KATE	*(on phone)* Jackson. Thirteen Ragnarok Drive.
	(off phone) Where's my coffee?
ANDREW	You said . . . Here.
KATE	*(on phone)* Thirteen! Rag-na-rok. Drive. Collect. Now!
CHARLIE	Dad?
ANDREW	What?
CHARLIE	My followers want to know what underwear you wear.
ANDREW	None of their business.
KATE	Tesco. Trunks. Three-pack every six months.
CHARLIE	What size?
KATE	L. Probably needs XL now.
ANDREW	Did you have to tell her/him? *(depending on actor playing Charlie)*
KATE	S/He'd lose a lot of his/her base otherwise.

Doorbell: KATE opens door to COURIER (B)

COURIER	Jackson?
KATE	Yes.

COURIER gives KATE an envelope

COURIER	Stand back. *(takes photo)* Thank you. Bye.

COURIER exits

KATE	It's for you.
ANDREW	I'm not expecting anything. Who's it from?
KATE	Open it.
CHARLIE	*(looking at phone, laughs)* Yeah, right!
KATE	What?
CHARLIE	PartyPooper says they're cheaper at ASDA.
	Can I get a photo, Dad? You in your knickers? Might get another few hundred followers if you do a Dad pose.
ANDREW	It's a form.
KATE	What for?
ANDREW	To claim for the package they lost.
KATE	Which one?
ANDREW	The empty one they sent to test the system to see where the previous one went missing.
KATE	Did they ever find it?
ANDREW	Which one? The test one or the original one?
KATE	Either.
ANDREW	No idea.
KATE	Well, you'd better fill out the form anyway. Might as well get compensation.
CHARLIE	Mum.

KATE   What? You're not getting me in my underwear.

CHARLIE   Course not, that would be sexist. How much do you pay for Dad's?

KATE   Don't remember.

Doorbell: ANDREW opens door to COURIER (A)

COURIER   Jackson?

ANDREW   Yes.

COURIER   Pick up a package.

KATE   This one. *(her samples)*

COURIER   I can't take that. It hasn't been sealed.

ANDREW   I'll find some sellotape.

KATE   I have to get ready.

COURIER   No time. Stand back.

COURIER takes a photo of ANDREW while KATE exits

ANDREW   What's that for?

COURIER   Proves you haven't given me anything. Bye.

COURIER exits

ANDREW   Goodbye.

CHARLIE   Dad?

ANDREW   What?

CHARLIE   Out of five, how do you rate your what-do-you-call-them, underwear?

ANDREW   Depends how far they ride up.

CHARLIE   Great answer!

ANDREW   If my underwear is earning you money, I want twenty percent.

CHARLIE   Have your people call my people.

ANDREW exits with his paperwork

CHARLIE taps / reacts to phone

Doorbell

CHARLIE   Mum!

Doorbell

CHARLIE   Dad!

Doorbell

CHARLIE sighs, gets up and opens door to COURIER (C)

COURIER   Chaudhury?

CHARLIE   What?

COURIER   Is your name Chaudhury?

CHARLIE   Do I look like a Chaudhury?

COURIER   That's racist. Watch it or you'll be on our blacklist.

CHARLIE   Whatever.

COURIER   Know someone called Chaudhury?

CHARLIE   No.

COURIER   Take this package for them?

COURIER gives CHARLIE package

CHARLIE   Wait!

COURIER takes photo

CHARLIE   What's that for?

COURIER   To prove you're not Mr Chaudhury.

CHARLIE   So take it back!

KATE enters

COURIER	Can't. It's been delivered. I'll put it In the system for recall.
KATE	You can take this back. *(her samples)*
COURIER	Not our company. Anyway, it's not closed properly. Gotta go.

COURIER exits

ANDREW enters

KATE	Got my sellotape?
ANDREW	What?
KATE	For my parcel.
ANDREW	Sorry. Forgot.
	This form.
KATE	What about it?
ANDREW	What date didn't it arrive?
KATE	What didn't arrive?
ANDREW	The package. Not the original one, the test one, the empty one.
KATE	I don't remember.
ANDREW	*(reading the form)* Was I in or out? Who was authorised to receive the package if I was out? Was it insured? Was there a designated safe place? A contact number?
KATE	The empty package?
ANDREW	Yes.
KATE	I don't know.
ANDREW	I have to put something down or I don't get compensation.
KATE	For something that didn't exist and didn't belong to you?

ANDREW	Yes.
KATE	How much are they offering?
ANDREW	As much as it was insured for. How much do you think?
KATE	Put down a thousand pounds.
ANDREW	Was it insured for that much?
KATE	It is now.

Doorbell

KATE	You go, Charlie.
CHARLIE	I'm busy.

ANDREW opens the door to COURIER (B)

COURIER	Charlie Jackson.
CHARLIE	*(leaps up)* That's me.
COURIER	Smile.
CHARLIE	What?
COURIER	*(taking photo)* New policy. If customers don't smile I lose my bonus.
CHARLIE	How's this?
COURIER	It'll do.

COURIER exits

CHARLIE	Wa-hey!
ANDREW	What is it?
CHARLIE	My new sex toy.
ANDREW	Where do you get your sense of humour?
CHARLIE	Who says I'm joking?

ANDREW   It had better not be illegal. Or pornographic. Or
                    drug-related. Explosive. Violent. Expensive.

CHARLIE   Relax. It's all of those.

CHARLIE exits

ANDREW   These columns. I have to fill them in. Product
                    Name. Description. Colour. Manufacturer.
                    Packaging. Shipping. Recycling. What's that
                    asterisk? "Labour costs not included".

KATE   We're still talking about the empty test package,
                    aren't we?

ANDREW   I think so - or it could be the original that went
                    missing. And now I remember, that was a
                    replacement for one I sent back because it was
                    the wrong size or the wrong colour or came with
                    instructions in Japanese.

KATE   What was the wrong size or wrong colour?

ANDREW   I've forgotten.

KATE   Ignore it. Forget the whole thing. Who needs to
                    collect insurance on an empty parcel anyway?

ANDREW   Can't do that. Down there in the small print it
                    says that failure to return this form may result in
                    all courier services being withdrawn from this
                    address and all personnel registered therein, by
                    this, associated, and all competing companies.

                    In short, if we don't claim for something we
                    didn't order and didn't receive we'll be blacklisted
                    and never sent another parcel again.

KATE   Sounds reasonable. Better fill it in. Here's a pen.

Doorbell: ANDREW opens the door to COURIER (C)

ANDREW   You were just here.

COURIER   No, I wasn't.

ANDREW	Yes, you were.
COURIER	All right, you got me. Different company, but don't tell them. I need the money.
	Pick up a package for Chaudhury.
ANDREW	Who?
COURIER	Is your name Chaudhury?
ANDREW	No.
COURIER	So give me the package for Chaudhury. It isn't yours.
ANDREW	I don't have a package for Chaudhury.

COURIER takes a photograph

ANDREW	I thought photos were only for deliveries
COURIER	Nah. Proves you don't have the package.
ANDREW	Don't you need me to smile?
COURIER	That's our competitors. We don't care.

COURIER exits

CHARLIE enters

CHARLIE	Anything for me?
ANDREW	Expecting another delivery?
CHARLIE	There's always something. Stuff my followers send me. Rubbish, most of it.
ANDREW	They wanted a parcel for Chaudhury.
CHARLIE	This one?
ANDREW	Where did that come from?
	(at door) Hey, come back!

COURIER (C) enters

COURIER   You're lucky I hadn't gone. I'm on a tight
                 schedule.

ANDREW   We found the package for Chaudhury.

COURIER   Not on my list.

ANDREW   You were just here asking for it.

COURIER   Was on my list. Isn't now. Logged it as not found.
                 Company'll get back to the customer. They'll sort
                 out a replacement. Covered by insurance.
                 Probably.

ANDREW   So what do we do with this?

COURIER   My advice? Keep it, throw it out, sell it on ebay.

COURIER takes a photograph

ANDREW   What the hell was that for?

COURIER   To prove you didn't give me anything.

COURIER exits

CHARLIE   I found the sellotape. Can I get back to work?

KATE seals her samples, taps the phone

ANDREW   You work?

CHARLIE   I haven't posted anything in ten minutes. My
                 followers are deserting me. Any ideas?

KATE   How much will you pay me?

CHARLIE   Mum, always the businesswoman. I learn from
                 the best.

KATE   I'm late. Will you drive me?

ANDREW   Why can't you?

KATE   No time to park.

ANDREW   I have a deadline.

CHARLIE   Come on, Dad. Artists don't have deadlines. And
                     Mum really doesn't want me driving her.

ANDREW   All right. Give me five minutes

Doorbell: KATE opens the door to COURIER (A)

COURIER   Charlie Jackson? *(hands over package)*

CHARLIE   That's me. Do I need to smile?

COURIER   Don't remember. Which job is this? Why not? Go
                     ahead. That the best you can do?

ANDREW   How many photos have you got on there?

COURIER   None; they're automatically deleted on this
                     device after they go to the office. Privacy
                     regulations.

ANDREW   What does the office do with them?

COURIER   Dunno. Keep them forever, I suppose. Have a
                     great day.

COURIER exits

ANDREW   Going to tell us what that one is?

CHARLIE   Soon as I soundproof my room.

CHARLIE exits

Doorbell: KATE opens door to COURIER (C)

COURIER   Jackson? Sign here.

KATE   No photo?

COURIER   No. We maintain the old-fashioned tradition that
                     has provided our customers with personalised
                     five-star service since our first delivery.

ANDREW   When was that?

COURIER   Six weeks ago.

COURIER exits

ANDREW   Who's it for?

KATE   "The Jackson Family."

ANDREW   Open it.

KATE   Did you order any of this?

ANDREW   No. You?

TOGETHER   Charlie!!

CHARLIE enters

CHARLIE   What?

KATE   What's all this stuff? Clothes. Electronics - I've no
                  idea what they're for.

CHARLIE   Why ask me?

KATE   A voucher for tantric healing.

CHARLIE   I'll have that.

KATE   A thousand pounds off our next car. Kitchenware.
                  God knows what else. What've you been up to?

CHARLIE   It's nothing to do with me.

ANDREW   I've found the dispatch note. It's all free.

KATE   Free?

ANDREW   Loyalty programme.

KATE   Which one? Amazon? Argos? Alibaba?

CHARLIE   Facebook? Instagram? Tik Tok? Google?

KATE   Ocado? DPD? B&Q? Netflix?

ANDREW   Doesn't say. Just "To the Jackson family, in
                  appreciation of your custom."

CHARLIE   That must be me. I order more stuff than you two
                  put together.

Doorbell: ANDREW opens door to COURIER (B)

COURIER	Andrew Jackson?
ANDREW	Yes.
COURIER	Like the seventh President of the United States? In office 1829 to 1837?
ANDREW	So I hear.
COURIER	A good guy. He founded the Democratic Party.
ANDREW	Did he?
COURIER	But a bad guy. He signed the Indian Removal Act.
ANDREW	I didn't know that.
KATE	You've got time for chit-chat?
COURIER	New policy. All drivers have to develop meaningful relationships with their customers. Swap recipes, chat about football, hobbies, that kind of thing. Anyway, Andrew Jackson, I have an envelope for you. Sign here.
ANDREW	Sign? Since when?
COURIER	New policy. Keeping up our with the competitors. Need a photo too.
ANDREW	With or without smile?
COURIER	Don't remember. Try both. Cheers.
	Catherine Jackson?
KATE	Yes?
COURIER	Andrew Jackson's wife was Rachel. Can't talk about history. Which team do you support?
KATE	Same as you.
COURIER	That's a coincidence. Pity about last week, isn't it?
KATE	That offside. The ref was blind.

COURIER	Wasn't he just? Anyway, can't stand here chatting all day. Envelope for you. Sign and photo.
	Charlie Jackson?
CHARLIE	That's me.
COURIER	Hey, you're that influencer!
CHARLIE	Yup.
COURIER	The one who eats dog and cat food and roadkill.
CHARLIE	No, I'm the one who . . .
COURIER	You should follow them. They're great.
	That's not a smile.
	Before I go, has my visit been satisfactory? Please visit Trustpilot and Tripadvisor and rate my performance for the chance to win free delivery of one item weighing not more than one kilo and with dimensions no greater than fifteen centimetres by twenty centimetres by fifty centimetres to any country in the world of your choice that is not currently involved in armed conflict or subject to severe flooding, heatwaves or volcanic activity. Terms and conditions apply.
ANDREW	Tripadvisor?
COURIER	I made the trip out here, didn't I? Take my photo, will you?
KATE	Why?
COURIER	To prove I was here. A pleasure working with you. Bye.

COURIER exits

ANDREW	We've all got the same. Some kind of contract.
CHARLIE	Boring!

ANDREW	It knows my full name, date of birth, height and weight.
KATE	That bit's wrong. I've lost two kilos since Christmas.
CHARLIE	Who's it from?
KATE	The Amalgamated British Courier Delivery Export Federation Group.

ANDREW's voice fades as the lighting slowly fades. While he speaks there is a speeded-up mime of the family's day: the doorbell rings more and more frequently as the COURIER [A, B, C in rotation] delivers more and more parcels, occasionally taking photographs or signatures or holding a silent conversation, and always failing to take back the ones that the family do not want. By total blackout the stage is almost completely covered in parcels under or behind which the family are buried.

| ANDREW | "To ensure excellent service from our members and colleagues, all customers are henceforward required to fulfil the following conditions in order to continue receiving packages ordered online, by telephone, in person or through methods and means otherwise unspecified or as yet created, designed or invented from now until the end of time. |

"First, ensure that a household member is present at the primary entrance from the hours of six am to eleven pm. Failure to answer arrival of the courier, which may be signified by not fewer than one and not more than three knocks on the door, window or side panel or by pressing an available bell or intercom button, with or without camera connected or otherwise to a security system for not fewer than one and not more than three seconds . . . "

.

SURREAL / FUTURISTIC

UMM KULTHUM

CAST

SHE   HE

probably both 20s

SHE   Come in.

HE   Are you sure?

SHE   Why not?

HE   You trust me?

SHE   Do you trust me?

HE   Of course.

SHE   So?

HE   You can't be too careful.

SHE   Yes, you can.

HE   All right, I'm in.

SHE   Welcome.

HE   Quiet.

SHE   Is that a problem?

HE   No, I'm just not used to it.

SHE   What's your place like?

HE   Not like this. Grubby. I share.

SHE   I don't. I couldn't.

HE   You're lucky.

SHE   I worked hard to get here.

HE   What do you do?

SHE   Civil service.

HE   What department?

SHE   Does it matter?

HE   Suppose not.

SHE   You?

HE   Between jobs.

SHE   What were you?

HE   Barman.

SHE   I see. What happened?

HE   I quit.

SHE   Because?

HE   The customers. Always talking. Shouting at each other, asking me questions, flirting.

SHE   That's a problem?

HE   When they're serious. They often were.

SHE   So were we flirting?

HE   Just now?

SHE   In the cafe.

HE   I don't know.

SHE   You started talking.

HE   Nothing else to do. No-one else to talk to. Too quiet.

SHE   So quiet is a problem?

HE   Not now. Don't know why, but it was there.

                You could have ignored me.

SHE   You looked sad.

HE   You were taking pity on me?

SHE	You looked cool and sad. Were you?
HE	Cool? Or sad? Isn't everyone sad?
SHE	Pretty much.
HE	But not you.
SHE	Perhaps I hide it.
HE	What's that on the walls?
SHE	Carpet. Thick, shaggy carpet.
HE	Strange place to put it. Do you walk on it?
SHE	Hey, humour!
HE	Sometimes.
SHE	I like your smile.
HE	I like yours. Why the carpet?
SHE	You said it was quiet. Sometimes I like quiet.
HE	Sometimes?
SHE	Sometimes. Come closer.
HE	Like this?
SHE	Like this. Got a girlfriend?
HE	No.
SHE	Boyfriend?
HE	No.
SHE	Significant other?
HE	No.
SHE	But you share a flat.
HE	Yes.
SHE	You got parents?
HE	One of each.

SHE	Unusual. Does it work?
HE	When I'm not with them. You?
SHE	What?
HE	All the same questions.
SHE	No. No. No. No. I'm not sure.
HE	You're not sure?
SHE	About my parents. There were two, very similar. We didn't get on.
HE	Why not?
SHE	Very strict.
HE	In what way?
SHE	The New Way.
HE	Ah.
SHE	Yours?
HE	Law-abiding.
SHE	Every law?
HE	Most.
SHE	Exceptions?
HE	Intoxicants.
SHE	They smoked?
HE	Claimed not to. I believed them until I was ten.
SHE	And you?
HE	Smoke? Sometimes. Seems pointless.
SHE	Why?
HE	It's an escape. Where are you escaping to? And you always come back. Do you smoke?

SHE	No.
HE	Inject? Anything?
SHE	Not now.
HE	What did you?
SHE	Doesn't matter.
HE	How do you get your kicks?
SHE	Where did that phrase come from?
HE	My father. Never knew what it meant.

Beat

SHE	We're still talking.
HE	I'm nervous.
SHE	Don't be.

SHE kisses him. He responds. They pull back and look into each other's eyes

SHE	My kicks . . .
HE	This?
SHE	Sometimes.

They kiss again

HE	You thought I was a virgin.
SHE	I wasn't sure.
HE	Are you now?
SHE	And me?
HE	You're not a virgin.
SHE	I'm a philosopher.
HE	What?
SHE	I think.

HE   Don't we all?

SHE   Not usually. Thoughts float through our heads.
              Sometimes they stick.

HE   So I'm an airhead.

SHE   I didn't say that.

HE   But you're thinking it.

SHE   No. You're thinking I'm thinking it.

HE   What are you thinking, about me?

SHE   I'm thinking you're sexy and innocent and I want to
              explore you.

HE   Explore me?

SHE   All of you.

HE   You sound like a pervert.

SHE   Define perversion.

HE   Something . . . I don't know . . . wrong, illegal, evil.

SHE   If you think I'm evil, you should leave.

HE   No, I'm curious. And you are . . .

They kiss again, each time getting more intimate

SHE   Tell me, what sounds do you like?

HE   Sounds?

SHE   Sounds.

HE   Like doorbells? Like traffic? People's voices? Machines?

SHE   Whatever. Anything.

HE   I never thought about it; they're just sounds.

SHE   How about smells? Bleach? Coffee? Farts?

HE   I don't like farts. Does anyone?

SHE	So what sounds don't you like?
HE	Loud, jarring.
SHE	People talking?
HE	It depends. Some people have nice voices. Like you.
SHE	Nice? Give me another word.
HE	I can't think of one.
SHE	Smooth, seductive, deep, authoritative, melodious . . .
HE	Mel – what?
SHE	Melodious.
HE	I don't understand.
SHE	What about singing?
HE	What's that?
SHE	Singing. *She sings a few notes*
HE	That sounds . . .
SHE	That sounds what? Pleasant?
HE	Yes, no, I don't know.
SHE	Musical instruments?
HE	What are they?
SHE	Instruments to make music.
HE	What's music?

SHE sings a few notes

HE	What're you doing? Isn't that . . .
SHE	Impossible? Illegal? Not the first. Probably the second.

Again SHE sings

HE	You're making me . . .
SHE	Nervous? How about this?

SHE continues to sing, produces a musical instrument and plays it. He is confused, uncertain, entranced.

HE   What's that?

SHE   [name of instrument]

HE   What does it do?

SHE   This. *She plays more* Do you like it?

HE   It's strange. I'm not sure. Do more. Yes.

HE closes his eyes

SHE   Now you're listening. Now it's enchanting you.

After a while

HE   Where did you get it?

SHE   From my grandfather. He hid it, during the Silence.
            Gave it to me. My birthmother never knew.

HE   The Silence?

SHE   They are – forgive the pun – silent about it in schools.

HE   I think I heard something about it.

SHE   That's ironic. The whole point was to hear nothing. A
            world without music. A world with no distractions.
            They even banned videos for a time.

HE   Who did?

SHE   Not who, what. The algorithms. Once the virus was let
            loose, nothing could be broadcast, reproduced or
            disseminated that had any melody or harmony . . .

HE   What?

SHE   Terms to do with music. Everything had to be flat,
            monotonous. It fed into the culture. Music became
            evil. Laws prevented people singing, even penalised
            parents for singing lullabies.

HE   Singing what? You're going too fast for me. All this . . .

SHE   You're right. It's a fantasy. I'm making it up. There's no such thing as music or singing. They're even more fantastic than zombies and killer robots. The only sounds are speech and traffic and machines. Even the birds don't sing any more.

HE   Birds are extinct. We don't know what noise they made.

SHE   Chirping. Warbling. Singing.

HE   Make that sound – again. Singing.

SHE sings

HE   It's . . .

SHE   It's what?

HE   I don't know. It's like a drug. It makes me feel . . . excited. Afraid.

SHE   Years ago, it was nothing special. Everyone could do it. Almost everyone. Some better than others. That's what I heard. Imagine a world where everyone sang. Maybe it never happened. Maybe it's a myth, Fake News. Nothing is true.

            You shouldn't have come. It was a mistake. You're looking at me like you think I'm crazy.

HE   I think you're . . . Can I kiss you again?

SHE   To stop me talking?

HE   Just to kiss.

He kisses her, at first uncertain then with some passion

SHE   You don't think I'm crazy?

HE   I don't care. Or if you are crazy, I like.

They kiss

SHE   Before we go on, let me do one thing. Let me do many
             things, but first . . .

SHE produces/ finds a cassette / vinyl / CD player and turns it on. The
overture to a song from Umm Kulthum begins to play. HE is
transfixed.

HE   What is this?

SHE   Music. From Egypt. A country that no longer exists.
             Listen.

Umm Kulthum begins to sing; SHE places his hand on her breast.

SHE   That is the human voice. It comes from within here.

HE   That's you? You can do that?

HE is torn between desire for her and rapture at the music.

SHE   If only. No, it's a woman singing in a language that has
             long been forgotten. Her name was Umm Kulthum.

HE   Umm Kulthum.

SHE   Your life will never be the same again.

SURREAL / FUTURISTIC

NOTHING TO BE DONE

CAST
G

MRS G   OLD LADY   YOUNG MAN   STRANGER
RAILWAY OFFICIAL   POTTS   LACKEY

*The stage is bare except for an anonymous bench: the atmosphere is
1950s.*

G	I'm off, dear.
MRS G	Got everything?
G	I think so.
MRS G	Bowler?
G	Yes.
MRS G	Umbrella?
G	Yes.
MRS G	Briefcase?
G	Yes.
MRS G	Handkerchief?
G	Yes.
MRS G	Sandwiches?
G	Yes.
MRS G	Flask?
G	Yes.
MRS G	Carnation?
G	*(pause)* No.
MRS G	No carnation?

G   No.

MRS G   Nothing to be done.

             What time will you be home?

G   Same as usual, dear.

MRS G   What time is your appointment?

G   They'll be there all day.

MRS G   They?

G   Two gentlemen.

MRS G   I see.

             It's haddock for dinner.

G   Delicious, dear. Goodbye.

MRS G   Goodbye.

MRS G exits and is replaced by three people waiting in a clearly defined queue.

G   Good morning.

OLD LADY   Good morning.

YOUNG MAN   Morning.

G   *(to STRANGER)* Good morning.

STRANGER   Ah, good morning.

G   We haven't met before.

STRANGER   No.

G   It's usually the same people at this time of the morning.

STRANGER   Ah.

G   We say good morning to each other.

STRANGER   I see.

OLD LADY   It's a friendly gesture.

STRANGER	Indeed.
OLD LADY	*(looking at the YOUNG MAN)* Although some of us don't always remember.
G	Well, youth must have its fling.
OLD LADY	Off to work, Mr G?
G	Same as every morning, Mrs Brown.
	How's the bank, Tommy?
YOUNG MAN	Still there, Mr G.
G	Glad to hear it.
	What work are you in, sir/madam?
STRANGER	I am indeed. In work. Working. At a job. Earning money.
G	What exactly do you do?
STRANGER	I'm not sure. But it's work. All day. With a break for lunch of course.
G	Of course.
STRANGER	And half days on Saturday. Whenever that is.

Silence

OLD LADY	The bus is late.
G	It's never late.
YOUNG MAN	Yes, it is. It was late yesterday.
G	Was it? I don't remember.
YOUNG MAN	Three minutes late.
G	*(to OLD LADY)* Was it?
OLD LADY	I'm not sure. I'm getting old, you see. My memory isn't what it was. *(to STRANGER)* Is yours?

55

STRANGER   My what?

OLD LADY   Your memory. Is your memory what it was?

STRANGER   Surely no-one's memory is what it was? My memory today is different from yesterday because today I remember things from yesterday that I hadn't begun to remember yesterday because they hadn't yet happened. And my memory today also differs from yesterday because I have forgotten today some things that I remembered yesterday, so, no, whether today, yesterday or tomorrow, my memory isn't what it was or what it will be. Is yours?

OLD LADY   Is my what?

Silence

G   I wonder when the bus will arrive.

YOUNG MAN   You in a hurry?

G   I have a train to catch.

OLD LADY   From the station?

G   Yes, from the station. Most trains stop there and those that don't stop can't be caught.

YOUNG MAN   What time is your train?

G   Ten minutes after the bus arrives at the station.

YOUNG MAN   But the bus is already several minutes late.

OLD LADY   Why are you taking the train?

G   I have an appointment. With two gentlemen.

YOUNG MAN   What time?

G   It doesn't matter. They will be there all day.

OLD LADY   *(to the STRANGER)* What time do you have to be at work?

STRANGER   I don't know, but I'll know when I get there.

YOUNG MAN   Where do you work?

STRANGER   I'm not sure, but I'll know when I get there.

OLD LADY   It's good to know that something is certain in this uncertain world, don't you agree, Mr G?

G   Oh, yes, I agree.

Silence

YOUNG MAN   I don't think the bus is coming.

STRANGER   I see.

OLD LADY   Nothing to be done.

STRANGER   Perhaps we should walk.

OLD LADY   I don't like to walk.

YOUNG MAN   Walking looks like the only solution.

Shall we walk?

OLD LADY   If we must.

STRANGER   In what direction?

YOUNG MAN   Just follow me.

G   Good bye, Mrs Brown.

OLD LADY   Goodbye, Mr G.

G   Goodbye, Tommy.

YOUNG MAN   Goodbye, Mr G.

G   *(to STRANGER)* Goodbye, er . . .

STRANGER   Goodbye.

STRANGER, YOUNG MAN and OLD LADY walk off in different directions. G looks around, looks in his briefcase, straightens his tie. RAILWAY OFFICIAL enters.

OFFICIAL   You've just missed your train.

G   I thought so.

OFFICIAL Was it important?

G   I have an appointment.

OFFICIAL At what time?

G   The time is not important. Tomorrow if not today.

OFFICIAL I see

G   When is the next train?

OFFICIAL That's a good question.

G   Thank you.

Silence

G   Is there an answer?

OFFICIAL There's usually an answer. To most questions. Some questions have no answers.

G   Is that true?

OFFICIAL There's another question.

G   That's true.

OFFICIAL The question is whether the answer to a question is an unquestionable answer or an answer that can be questioned. Such as the existence of God.

G   That's not a question.

OFFICIAL That's true. Some questions can only be answered by God, but if there is no God, does that mean those questions are unanswerable, or that those questions do not exist?

G   That is a question.

OFFICIAL That's true.

G   Does it have an answer?

OFFICIAL	There's usually an answer. To most questions. Some questions have no answers.
G	You said that before.
OFFICIAL	That's true.

Silence

G	When is the next train?
OFFICIAL	To where you're going?
G	Yes.
OFFICIAL	You're asking me for a definite time.
G	Yes.
OFFICIAL	For a specific train.
G	Yes.
OFFICIAL	To a specific town.
G	Yes.
OFFICIAL	Where you have an appointment.
G	No.
OFFICIAL	No?
G	From the next station I have further to go.
OFFICIAL	To your destination.
G	Yes.
OFFICIAL	But not by train.
G	No.
OFFICIAL	Then how?
G	I'm not sure. I'll find out when I get there.

Silence

G   When is the next train to the station to where I'm
                going and from where I will proceed by a method as
                yet undetermined to my final destination for my
                appointment with two gentlemen who are waiting
                for me which may happen any time today? If I get
                there today. Otherwise it will be tomorrow.

OFFICIAL   It's been cancelled.

G   The appointment has been cancelled?

OFFICIAL   The train has been cancelled.

G   I see.

OFFICIAL   Nothing to be done.

RAILWAY OFFICIAL walks away

*G looks around, sits down, opens his briefcase and takes out a
sandwich and the flask. He pours himself tea and takes a bite from
his sandwich.*

*Enter POTTS wearing a bowler hat and LACKEY carrying a heavy bag,
a folding stool, a picnic basket, a greatcoat and a bowler hat.
LACKEY stands back and does not put his burden down.*

POTTS   Good evening, sir.

G   *(embarrassed, putting away his sandwich and flask
                and standing up)* Is it evening already?

POTTS   Undoubtedly it is evening. It is always evening
                somewhere and there is always endless night.
                Somewhere. Meanwhile the sun shines at noon all
                day as it crosses the world or, as many would have it,
                the world crosses it, or something similar.

G   That's true.

POTTS   And so again I say good evening.

G   Good evening to you. But it isn't evening now, here?

POTTS   Of course not, sir, whatever gave you that

impression? Look out at the sky, blue with clouds scuttering by, and over there – I advise you not to look directly, sir, to protect your eyes – shines Phoebus the Sun.

G   That is a relief.

POTTS   A relief, sir? A relief from what?

G   From worry, concern. I have an appointment today that I don't wish to miss.

POTTS   What time would that be?

G   The time isn't important but I promised them today.

POTTS   Them?

G   The two gentlemen I have to meet.

POTTS   I see.

     And now you are waiting . . .

G   For the next train. Which is cancelled, but perhaps not the one after.

POTTS   Does anyone know?

G   I assume someone knows, but not me.

     I would have preferred to travel this morning.

POTTS   So would we all, those of us who travel.

G   Early is usually better than late.

POTTS   I can think of circumstances when it isn't.

G   You may be right.

POTTS   I usually am.

G   On the other hand, late is always better than never.

POTTS   I can think of circumstances when it isn't.

G   You may be right.

POTTS   I usually am.

Silence

POTTS   My name is Potts, sir.

G   How do you do, Mr Potts.

POTTS   I said Potts.

G   So did I.

POTTS   You do not know me?

G   No, I don't. Do you know me?

POTTS   No, I don't but that does not matter.

G   I don't suppose it does.

POTTS   Potts! Potts! Potts!

G   Potts. Potts. Potts.

      And your companion?

POTTS   My companion? What companion?

G   The gentleman at the door.

POTTS   The gentleman?

G indicates LACKEY

POTTS   That is no gentleman. That is my lackey.

G   Good morning, or good evening, Mr Lackey.

POTTS   He cannot hear you.

G   I am sorry to hear that. Is he deaf?

POTTS   I said he cannot hear you.

G   And I asked if he was deaf.

POTTS   He is not wearing his hat.

G   I can see that.

POTTS   Perhaps you should give him his hat.

G	He has his hat.
POTTS	But not on his head.
G	That is true.
POTTS	Your hat is on your head as mine is on mine.
G	That is true.
POTTS	But his hat is in his hand.
G	Also true.
POTTS	And so he cannot hear. Perhaps you should put his hat on his head?
G	I?
POTTS	You don't expect me to do so?
G	Well . . .
POTTS	Put his hat on his head.

G approaches LACKEY and carefully and gently prises the hat from his hands. As he does so, all the other things LACKEY is carrying fall. No-one moves to pick them up. G balances the bowler hat precariously on LACKEY's head.

POTTS	Well done, sir!
G	Thank you.
	And now?
POTTS	Now he can hear and he can think.
G	Think?
POTTS	Think. *(to LACKEY)* Think!

LACKEY does not move

POTTS	Now you see.
G	See what?
POTTS	He is thinking.

G   How do you know?

POTTS   Because his hat is on his head. He only thinks when
           his hat is on his head.

G   What is he thinking?

POTTS   How should I know?

G   Don't you ask him?

POTTS   I did once. I didn't like what he said.

G   What did he say?

POTTS   I don't remember. It was long ago. Perhaps
           yesterday.

G   Perhaps he is thinking something different today.

POTTS   That is a possibility.

G   You could ask him.

POTTS   I could. So could you.

G   Oh no, I couldn't. We haven't been introduced.

POTTS   That is true.

           Lackey! Are you thinking?

LACKEY   I am thinking.

POTTS   What are you thinking?

LACKEY   Is it raining no it isn't am I tired yes I am

G   Is that all?

LACKEY   When did I last eat when will I eat again this man is
           this man is this man is

G   He seems to have stopped.

POTTS   He usually thinks better when given a subject.

G   Such as?

POTTS	Such as the composition of light or seventeenth century poetry or the personality of dogs away from their owners or how to make rhubarb pie.
LACKEY	First catch your rhubarb in the early morning with John Donne's sonnets can be detected at the lower end of the spectrum by certain breeds of canine with self-raising flour that is contrary to the 1843 Act of Recession except when John Donne, John Donne, John Donne his business without supervision . . .
POTTS	Stop!
LACKEY	. . . which is understandable if the library is open on Wednesdays without heating your oven to 200 degrees when . ..
POTTS	I said STOP!
LACKEY	. . . rhubarb is in season, rhubarb, rhubarb, rhubarb . . .

POTTS knocks LACKEY's hat to the floor. G picks it up, is not sure who to hand it to so holds onto it somewhat nervously.

G	I'm not sure I understood everything he said.
POTTS	He is getting out of control. Would you have rope in that briefcase?
G	I beg your pardon?
POTTS	Would you have rope in that briefcase?
G	I'm afraid I cannot divulge the contents but I assure you that there is no rope.
POTTS	A pity. I could use some rope. And a whip.
G	A whip. What for?
POTTS	One can always use rope. And a whip.
	You didn't tell me your name.
G	That is true.

POTTS   I told you my name was Potts. In fact it still is Potts. Tomorrow, unless it changes, it will be Potts again.

               The name is wrong. It's not appropriate. It doesn't give me gravitas. I'm thinking of changing it.

G   To what?

POTTS   *(ruminating)* Potts. . . Potts . . .

               He can dance, you know.

G   Who?

POTTS   My lackey. Would you like to see him dance?

G   It would pass the time.

POTTS   He's wearing the wrong boots.

G   Then another time.

POTTS   Another time.

G   Does he need music?

POTTS   No, but he must have the boots.

Silence

POTTS   Well, we must be on our way.

G   I'm afraid I can't join you.

POTTS   My lackey and me. The exclusive "we". You were not included.

G   I see.

POTTS   His hat, sir.

G   Ah yes. *(hands it to POTTS, who takes it reluctantly)*

POTTS   Lackey! Where is that whip? Lackey!!

LACKEY suddenly becomes active, picks up the various items he has dropped and moves them from hand to hand to arm as he tries to work out the most comfortable way of carrying them. Eventually he settles down.

POTTS   Time waits for no man.

G   Or woman.

POTTS is surprised by the sentiment

POTTS   Indeed, sir.

               (to LACKEY) Onward!

POTTS holds out LACKEY's hat. In taking it, LACKEY drops at least one item and there is some confusion while he picks it up and arranges everything he is carrying.

POTTS   *(to G)* Nothing to be done.

               (to LACKEY) Onward!

G watches LACKEY and POTTS walk off, then sits down, takes out the half-eaten sandwich and flask, pours himself tea and eats the sandwich.

RAILWAY OFFICIAL enters

OFFICIAL   Good evening.

G   Is it?

OFFICIAL   Good or evening?

G   Either.

OFFICIAL   It is evening.

G   Already?

OFFICIAL   Already. And it is good for me because it is time for me to go home. I hope it will also be good for you.

G   Will there be a train?

OFFICIAL   Not today. Tomorrow.

G   Can I wait here?

OFFICIAL   For what?

G   Tomorrow's train. I don't want to be late.

OFFICIAL	None of us do. Still, better late than never.
G	Is that true?
OFFICIAL	I can think of circumstances when it isn't. And it's better to be early than late.
G	So they say.
OFFICIAL	Although I can think of circumstances when it isn't.
	I have to lock up now.
G	Ah. *(finishes sandwich and returns flask to his briefcase)* Nothing to be done.
OFFICIAL	That is true.

G stands up, straightens his clothing. The RAILWAY OFFICIAL departs. The YOUNG MAN, OLD LADY and STRANGER arrive in a queue facing the opposite direction from before.

G	Good evening.
OLD LADY	Good evening.
YOUNG MAN	Evening.
STRANGER	Good evening.
OLD LADY	Back from work, Mr G?
G	Same as every evening, Mrs Brown.
YOUNG MAN	Get to your appointment?
G	I'm afraid not.
OLD LADY	They will be disappointed.
G	Who will?
OLD LADY	The gentlemen you were meeting.
G	Oh yes.
	How was the bank, Tommy?
YOUNG MAN	Still there, Mr G.

G   Glad to hear it.

                    And your work, sir/madam?

STRANGER   Yes, I did. Work.

OLD LADY   That's nice.

G   With a break for lunch?

STRANGER   I don't remember.

YOUNG MAN   The bus is late.

OLD LADY   It's never been late before.

YOUNG MAN   It is today.

OLD LADY   Better late than never.

STRANGER   I can think of circumstances when it isn't.

G   That's true.

YOUNG MAN   Nothing to be done.

STRANGER   Perhaps we should walk.

OLD LADY   I don't like to walk.

YOUNG MAN   Walking looks like the only solution.

G   I agree.

YOUNG MAN   Shall we walk?

OLD LADY   If we must.

STRANGER   In what direction?

YOUNG MAN   Just follow me.

G   Good bye, Mrs Brown.

OLD LADY   Goodbye, Mr G.

G   Goodbye, Tommy.

YOUNG MAN   Goodbye, Mr G.

G   *(to STRANGER)* Goodbye, er . . .

STRANGER   Goodbye.

STRANGER, YOUNG MAN and OLD LADY walk off in different directions. G does not move.

Mrs G enters

MRS G   Had a good day, dear?

G   Yes.

MRS G   How was your appointment?

G   I didn't get there.

MRS G   No? Will you go back tomorrow?

G   Yes.

MRS G   Will the two gentlemen be there?

G   I believe so.

MRS G   And the day after?

G   I believe so.

MRS G   Better late than never.

G   So they say, although I can think of circumstances when it isn't.

MRS G   *(taking / checking the items one by one)* Bowler. Brolly. Briefcase. Handkerchief. Flask. Did you enjoy the sandwiches?

G   Yes, dear.

MRS G   No carnation?

G   No.

MRS G   Nothing to be done.

             There's haddock for dinner.

G   Delicious, dear.

SURREAL / FUTURISTIC
HAND AND FOOT

CAST
MARY

RA   RH   HT   ST   LL   LF

VOICES ONE and TWO

SET
Ideally as here, but can be modified to space available

Upstage

MARY *asleep in a bed*

RA, RH (tied to each other)

HT

ST

LL, LF (tied to each other)

Downstage

On curtain up everyone is motionless and eyes closed except ST and HT, who is tapping out a regular beat; HT's tapping comes and goes and should be adapted to the production.

ST   Can you not stop that?

HT   You know I can't.

ST   Well, at least quieter.

HT   I'm always quieter, compared to some of the noises you make.

ST   You'll wake her up.

HT   All right.

HT taps more quietly; eventually unnoticed stops tapping altogether

ST   How long has it been?

HT   How long has what been?

ST   That we've been asleep.

HT   I never sleep.

ST   You know what I mean.

HT   I don't know.

ST   It feels like forever. (*stretches*) I can't remember the last
            time I ate. I feel as if I've shrunk. I know I've shrunk.

HT   Don't go on about it.

ST   I'm not going on. I need nourishment. It's a statement of
            fact.

HT   A fact that you are fond of repeating every time you're
            hungry.

ST   Well, I'm hungry now. I don't know how you keep going.

HT   If I didn't keep working, what would happen to you and
            everyone else? But you don't hear me complain.

ST   You do sometimes.

HT   Not as much as you. The noises you make . . .

ST   I have to remind her.

MARY groans and stirs

HT   Did you do that?

ST   No!

*MARY makes a slight movement at the same time as LL sits up in
horror and looks at LF*

LL   Who are you?

LF   Who are you?

LL   Where's my partner? Who are you?

LF   Who are you? I've never seen you before. What am I
            doing here? Where am I?

They begin fighting but with little strength and inconclusively

LL   You shouldn't be here. Go away. Get off me.

LF   Let me go. I don't want to be here. I want to be home.

HT   What's going on down there?

ST   How should I know?

HT   You're nearer than I am.

ST   That doesn't mean I know any more than you.

LL   Get off!

LF   Let me go!

After a few ineffectual blows LL and LF are exhausted

HT   Something's wrong.

ST   What do you mean something's wrong?

HT   I mean something's wrong. Everyone's asleep. Usually when she's asleep some of you move about. Even you spend half the night working.

ST   And you never sleep as you never tire of telling us.

HT   I have great responsibility, which I take very seriously.

ST   For which we're all very grateful(!)

HT   I should hope so.

Pause

LL and LF jostle each other

HT   What's going on? Hey, you down there! What's going on?

LL   Did she wake up?

HT   No.

LL   Well, she should. We've got an intruder.

ST   What do you mean, an intruder?

LL   My partner has gone. There's a stranger in her place.

HT	That's impossible.
LF	Let me go!
LL	Hear that? She's hitting me.
LF	Let me go!
ST	I've never heard that voice before. Who is it?
LL	I told you, an intruder.
ST	Get rid of her!
LL	How? We're tied. One minute I'm with my partner. Next I wake up and there's a stranger in her place and I can't get rid of her.
HT	*(tapping quickly)* I don't like the sound of this.
ST	Something must have happened.
LF	I want to go home! Jenny! Jenny!
ST	What's that?
LL	She's calling for Jenny.
ST	Who's Jenny?
HT	I don't like this. I don't like it at all.

MARY stirs but does not wake.

LF	I shouldn't be here!
LL	So go.
LF	I don't know how. I don't know where. I can't. We're tied together.
LL	Get off me!
LF	I can't be on my own.
LL	Get off!
LF	Where am I to go?

LL   Anywhere, but go! Go! Go!

LF   Jenny! Jenny!

ST   Who's this Jenny?

LL   I don't know, but this one's holding on tight, too tight.

LF   I'm going to stay here until Jenny comes for me.

LF clings tighter. LL's resistance fades

LL   You're hurting me.

LF   I don't care.

After a weak tussle, they both lie still

ST   Something's going on down there. We have to wake Mary.

HT   You do it. She hears you, never me.

ST jumps up and down and makes weird gurgling noises. HT taps faster and louder. MARY stirs but does not wake.

RH and RL come to life. ST's and HT's sounds underlie their dialogue.

RA   What's going on? Who are you?

RH   What?

RA   Who are you?

RH   Who are you? What's this *(the ties)*? Where am I?

RA   Where did you come from?

RH   Where did you come from? How did I get here? What's going on?

They each examine the ties between them.

RA   I don't know, but I don't like it. I don't like you.

RH   You don't know me.

RA   You're not my partner. You've taken her place.

RH   You're not my partner. I don't know how I got here. I don't want to be here.

RA   I want my partner back.

RH   And I want mine.

RA   At least we agree on something.

HT's tapping has died away

HT   What's going on over there?

RA   I've lost my partner. I've got a new one.

HT   What?

RA   I said I've lost my partner.

HT   Did you hear that?

ST   I did. What's happening to us?

HT   When did you lose her?

RA   I don't know. I was asleep and I woke up and this one was here. She doesn't want to be here.

RH   I don't. I want to be back with Jenny.

HT   Are you the new partner? What did you say?

RH   I don't want to be here. I want to be back with Jenny. I've been with Jenny all my life. I love Jenny and she loves me.

ST   Did you say Jenny?

RH   Yes!

ST   That's what the other one said.

RA   The other what?

HT   The other intruder.

RA   Where?

HT   Down below. There's an intruder who says she wants to go back to Jenny.

ST   What's happening to us?

HT   *(tapping faster)* Don't panic.

ST   It sounds as if you are.

RA   Isn't Mary awake?

RH   Who's Mary?

ST   No, she's been asleep for ages. We don't know how.
        Something's wrong.

HT   Two intruders, from Jenny.

RH   Who's Mary?

ST   Who is this Jenny?

RH   Jenny's wonderful. She's an artist. We make beautiful
        paintings together. She's just beginning to be successful.
        There's a major exhibition coming up next week. We're
        going to be there and it'll be fabulous. Who's Mary?

RA   Mary is everything to us. She's a mother with a beautiful
        boy. When we hold him and he smiles the world is
        perfect.

ST   It's not so perfect when his nappies have to be changed.

HT   Do I detect a bit of hypocrisy there?

ST   I'm not responsible for what goes on below.

HT   You certainly have input.

        Tell us more about Jenny and how you came to be here.

RA   And what have you done to my partner?

RH   I haven't done anything to your partner and I have no
        idea how I came to be here. Do you think I'd be here if I'd
        rather be with Jenny? Why would I want to be with a
        mother when I could be with a woman whose art is
        viewed by thousands?

77

HT	Mary isn't just a mother. She's a respected academic. An astrophysicist.
ST	Whatever that means. I've never understood it.
HT	None of us do. All that matters is that she does.

HT is tapping

RH	I miss Jenny. I miss my partner. I miss all the others. You sound like them but you're not the same. That beat *(HT's taps)* isn't right. Something's wrong.
ST	That's what we've been saying all along.
LL	*(weakly)* Help.
HT	What's going on down there?
LL	She's strangling me. The intruder.
HT	Can't you fight back?
LL	She's too strong.
HT	You down there, stranger, you said you were with Jenny.
LF	That's right. Where is she?
HT	We don't know, but there's another of you up here.
LF	What do you mean?
RH	I'm from Jenny, too.
LF	You are? How did you get here? Where are we?
RH	We're with someone called Mary.
LF	Who's Mary? Did you tell them about Jenny?
RH	Yes.
LF	We have to get out of here.
RH	How? I've got a new partner. I can't get free.
LF	So have I. She attacked me. I had to subdue her but I can't get free.

LL   I'm not well. I'm really not well.

HT   And if you're not well . . .

ST   It affects the rest of us.

RA   I feel faint.

A lethargy overcomes all the characters. HT taps slowly

VOICE ONE   The lab confirms it's toxoplasmosis.

VOICE TWO   Not unexpected but not helpful.

VOICE ONE   Treatment?

VOICE TWO   Amoxicillin. Check every six hours.

VOICE ONE   It's going in now.

MARY groans and moves. HT taps a little quicker then slowly back to normal

VOICE ONE   She should wake soon.

VOICE TWO   There's been significant trauma.

VOICE ONE   Accident and amputations.

VOICE TWO   Transplant of hand and foot.

VOICE ONE   At least her life was saved.

HT's tapping fades as the characters begin to move.

ST   I'm hungry.

HT   You must be feeling better.

ST   I suppose I am.

HT   How is everybody?

RA   Confused.

LL   Hurting.

LF   I let you go.

LL   Not completely.

LF	I feel better. I don't want to hurt you any more.
LL	Thank goodness for that.
RA	What happens now?
HT	We wait for Mary to wake up.
RA	Will that be soon?
ST	I hope so. I'm hungry.
HT	You keep saying that.
ST	I keep being hungry.
RA	Are you all right?
RH	I'm not sure.
RA	How do you feel?
RH	Sad. I don't think I'm going back to Jenny. I don't think she's there any more.
LF	I did. She must have gone and left us.
ST	Gone where?
RA	Where we'll all go in the end.
HT	You'll miss her.
RH	Terribly.
LF	At least you were part of her creativity. She did nothing with me except spent most of the day standing. At the end of the day my muscles always hurt.
LL	Mary's not like that. We walk around a bit but for hours at a time she'll put us up on a chair. If you're not careful you'll find yourself going to sleep in the middle of the afternoon. It's agony when she wakes us.
LF	I'll deal with it.
RA	You won't paint any more.
RH	I'll miss it. I was so proud of what we did.

HT   Perhaps Mary will go and see Jenny's exhibition. Bring them together.

ST   You're part of Mary now.

RA   Life will be very different.

HT   In some ways. Not all the time. Women are women and people are people. Everyone has a lot in common.

RA   You'll need to get used to typing. It'll take time, but she uses her other hand a lot.

RH   And I'll get to hold the baby.

RA   You'll get to hold the baby.

            You'll miss your partner.

RH   Not if you and I work well together.

RA   Let's try.

LL   Can we work together?

LF   I suppose so.

LL   You'll stop trying to hurt me?

LF   I already have.

LL   We're a new partnership. We depend on you up there.

HT   We'll do our best.

ST   As long as she gives me decent food, I'm here for the long haul.

RA   We all are.

RH   And me.

LF   And me.

MARY opens her eyes

VOICE ONE   You're awake.

MARY   Where am I?

VOICE ONE   You're in hospital. I'm afraid you had an accident but we think you'll fully recover . . .

SEX / VIOLENCE
THE RECKONING

CAST
CHRISTOPHER MARLOWE
INGRAM FRIZER
NICHOLAS SKERES
ROBERT POLEY
ELEANOR BULL
EDWIN

There have been many theories as to how and why
Christopher Marlowe died; some of them are repeated here.

An Elizabethan ale-house; MARLOWE, FRIZER, SKERES and POLEY
stretched out on chairs and benches.

MARLOWE	For sooth I am as tired as a dog that has tupped a dozen bitches.
FRIZER	And I as a man that has served a dozen wenches.
SKERES	Mistress Bull!
POLEY	And I as horse that has mounted a dozen mares.
MARLOWE	While in truth not one of us has stirred from this tavern all the long day and no bitch or wench or mare has received our kind attentions.
SKERES	Mistress Bull!
MARLOWE	Come, Master Ingram, tell us, of the three - bitch, wench or mare – which would give a man greatest pleasure?
FRIZER	What would I know of mounting dogs or horses?
MARLOWE	Thou art country-bred, where comely wenches are few and dogs and horses a-plenty.

FRIZER   And thou a Cambridge scholar where the rumps of
           boys are more tender than pork or mutton.

Enter BULL

BULL   What now, gentlemen? Are you not sated? Have you
           no homes to go to? Affairs of state or love to beckon
           you? Or will you stay till tomorrow's cock crows?

MARLOWE   My cock may yet crow today and so I loiter.

POLEY   Mistress Bull, wouldst thou rather four drunken fools
           pay thee for ale and fodder or sit in an empty tavern
           with none but thy servant for company?

BULL   Much greater company I would have if you four did
           not mock every stranger who would enter.

MARLOWE   Untrue, madam! Each face that presents itself at that
           door is beckoned in. We chase none away and yet
           they run.

BULL   They that run have better fortune than those who
           stay.

FRIZER   What meanst thou by that?

BULL   Master Skeres' smiling countenance has ensnared
           many who venture here.

SKERES   Ensnared, Mistress Bull?

BULL   You lend money for interest, an un-Christian act.

SKERES   My fee is is little. Wouldst thou enrich fat Jews and
           not good Christian men?

BULL   The man who places his mark against your bill may
           ne'er be free of debt.

MARLOWE   'Tis true, I've heard it said.

BULL   And you, Master Frizer, stand as witness, yet when
           both are charged with usury, lies and bribery set you
           free.

SKERES   A calumny!

BULL   And you, Master Poley? I would wager a butt of ale that you and Truth were never bedfellows, for from dawn to dusk deceit and lies are your constant companions.

POLEY   Take care, Mistress Bull, lest we take offence.

BULL   God's blood, sir, take no offence! I speak in jest. You pay me well enough to keep my counsel. What care I if fools and their money are soon parted?

POLEY   Indeed, we are the most honest and friendliest of fellows, as I will prove if thou wilt but sit upon my lap.

FRIZER   Or mine.

SKERES   Or mine.

MARLOWE   Or mine, indeed, although if truth be told, thou art a little ripe and I prefer my flesh thinner. But if thou wert to beg me . . .

BULL   I will beg for nothing, sir, except the reckoning for all the meat and ale that today has passed your hungry lips.

MARLOWE   And that shalt thou have, but first . . .

SKERES   . . . bring us more of your boiled mutton.

POLEY   And a jug of malmsey.

MARLOWE   No, two jugs.

FRIZER   And bread.

BULL   Nothing more?

MARLOWE   That will suffice. And at thy leisure send thy servant Edwin. I would have a word with him.

Exit BULL

MAR (cont)   Good friends, I would smoke but my pipe lies empty.
               Might you . . . ?

POLEY   Not I, dear Kit.

SKERES   Nor I.

POLEY   Nor I.

MARLOWE   What? Are ye callow youths? Know ye not that those
               that love not tobacco are fools?

FRIZER   Hast thou not another love? Oft have we heard thee
               praise the slender limbs of . . .

POLEY   Oft enough, indeed. I weary of that tale.

FRIZER   Then what shall we now?

SKERES   Why, wait upon the vittles.

FRIZER   And to amuse us till they come?

MARLOWE   Thou wilt have amusement?

POLEY   Amuse us, dear Kit. Our minds are slow and thine is
               quick.

FRIZER   And thou hast many tales to tell.

MARLOWE   My tales you have seen upon the stage.

SKERES   I have not seen them all.

POLEY   And those I saw I oft saw when deep in drink.
               Memory confuses battles on the stage with battles
               among the groundlings.

FRIZER   Your first, what was it?

MARLOWE   The Tragedie of Dido.

SKERES   Queen of Carthage? Thy work or Thomas Nashe's?

MARLOWE   Mine, all mine, save a word or two I allowed him.

POLEY   I saw it performed by the Children of the Chapel. A
               worthy play but curious.

MARLOWE   Curious, dear Robert?

POLEY   Curious. If I recall, Jupiter swore his love for
               Ganymede.

MARLOWE   As legend tells us.

FRIZER   As thy Edward did for young Gaveston.

MARLOWE   As history tells us.

SKERES   Leander's looks, thy poem tells us "were all that men
               desire." Men, not maidens.

MARLOWE   That line, it seems, hath pierced thy heart. What be
               thy point?

POLEY   That oft thy heroes turn from nature and against
               God's law.

MARLOWE   Against God's law, for sooth? Which law might that
               be? There are so many.

SKERES   That man should not lie with man.

MARLOWE   Then do not lie with me but tell me true, how often,
               when a youth, didst thou lie with another's wife? Or
               how oft dost thou, now married, lie with maid?

FRIZER   He has thee there, Nicholas Skeres. How oft hast
               thou broken God's laws?

SKERES   If I have sinned, I do repent.

POLEY   And sin no more?

MARLOWE   (laughs) Harken to his silence!

Enter BULL with ale and EDWIN with meat

MARLOWE   Tell me, Mistress Bull, which sin is greater, a man
               who gets a maid with bastard child or one who finds
               his pleasure in a boy's rump whence nothing comes
               but rich night soil?

BULL   God knows better than I the greater sin. For me there
               is but one that I despise.

87

SKERES   And that sin is . . . ?

BULL   To order ale and have no coin to pay it, to fill the belly when the pouch hangs empty.

POLEY   I do assure thee, Mistress Bull, my pouch hangs full, though what it holds is for no man and not for every woman.

BULL   Your humour, sir, is of the basest kind.

POLEY   Madam, with you, I may be base but always kind.

BULL   Hah!

Bull exits. All except MARLOWE eat, MARLOWE moves aside with EDWIN

MARLOWE   Stay a minute, Master Edwin.

EDWIN   Sir?

MARLOWE   Where is the boy Benjamin?

EDWIN   I know not.

MARLOWE   He lives here does he not?

EDWIN   He does.

MARLOWE   And shares your bed.

EDWIN   The nights are cold.

MARLOWE   Spring is upon us.

EDWIN   But winter lingers.

MARLOWE   When last I was here, young Benjamin besought my help to read and write.

EDWIN   What need has he of reading and writing?

MARLOWE   A servant who knows his letters soon finds advancement.

EDWIN   He needs not advancement nor letters nor the honeyed words you whisper in his ear.

MARLOWE   Yet he wants improvement, a nobler house in which
           to serve.

EDWIN   All he needs - a bed at night, a shirt on his back and
           bread on his plate - I give him. He is content.

MARLOWE   Content? He lives in fear of the rope with which thou
           lashest him.

EDWIN   Fear is the best teacher of errant lads.

MARLOWE   If that be the case, I am of a mind to give you fresh
           instruction. I tell thee, send me the boy. There is coin.
           There will be another for him.

EDWIN   I want not your coin, nor does he.

EDWIN spits and leaves; after a pause MARLOWE joins the others.

FRIZER   Tell me, Kit, where wast thou today?

MARLOWE   Why, Master Frizer, with you three since before
           noon. Dost not remember we met on London Bridge
           and wandered as aimless as mayflies to this sweet
           nesting-place?

SKERES   Some mayflies! Some nesting-place!

FRIZER   And before we met?

MARLOWE   Before?

FRIZER   Where wast thou?

MARLOWE   A-wandering. A-musing on my next play.

POLEY   What is the story?

MARLOWE   Ah, if only I knew, I would tell thee.

FRIZER   Wast thou perhaps at Whitehall?

SKERES   Whitehall?

POLEY   Summoned by the Queen?

MARLOWE   Alas, fair Gloriana does not concern herself with such
           as I.

FRIZER But her Council does, does it not?

POLEY The Privy Council?

MARLOWE What might the Privy Council want with me?

FRIZER Rumour says there is a warrant for thy arrest.

MARLOWE Rumour often lies. Rumour talks to hear her own voice. Rumour oft runs fast while Truth lies still asleep.

FRIZER And sometimes Rumour and Truth walk hand in hand.

POLEY Come, Kit, reveal thyself. What is Rumour and what is Truth?

MARLOWE '"What is truth?" said jesting Pilate. Rumour is Kit Marlowe blasphemes, is treasonous, without religion and cruel. You know me well, ask yourselves if that is Truth - and if it is, you share my company, do you also share my guilt?

SKERES God forfend that I be treasonous. There is no more loyal subject of Her Majesty than me.

FRIZER Nor I.

POLEY Nor I.

FRIZER And thou, Kit?

MARLOWE I cannot weigh my loyalty against others. Who knows who in this realm stands most fast against Gloriana's enemies? I only say that I wish Her Majesty long life, no harm and the great happiness of reigning over a peaceful and contented nation.

FRIZER Yet the Privy Council summons thee.

MARLOWE I serve gladly at the Council's service until it releases me. As yet it has not seen fit to do so, nor order me imprisoned in a Newgate cell.

SKERES   How knowst thou this, friend Frizer?

MARLOWE   I will answer that. Friend Frizer serves Sir Thomas
            Walsingham, a worthy knight, oft seen at court and,
            despite my many faults, my patron. Friend Frizer
            keeps his counsel on his situation as do I. In the
            common crowd Sir Thomas' reputation for intrigue
            invites much speculation and little illumination.

POLEY   But if Sir Thomas be your patron, why art thou
            subject to arrest?

MARLOWE   Arrest? What arrest? I come here freely and any of
            you may summon the Queen's Men to put me under
            charge.

SKERES   I have heard Rumour . . .

MARLOWE   Ah, Dame Rumour returns. What wares does she
            carry in her basket? Who will buy?

SKERES   Rumour that some there are that wear a double
            mask.

FRIZER   What mask?

SKERES   My Lord Bumpton wishes to learn My Lord
            Cumpton's business. My Lord Bumpton pays My Lord
            Cumpton's servant for news of his master's dealings.
            My Lord Cumpton's servant informs his master of the
            offer and so my Lord Cumpton offers a similar reward
            to learn of My Lord Bumpton's private affairs. Thus
            one man wears two masks and none can tell which, if
            either, is the true.

MARLOWE   And which am I, my dear Poley? Lord Bumpton or
            Lord Cumpton? Please not the servant. I have no
            temper for humility to one lord far less two.

SKERES   Dear Kit, I know not who thou art. Thou jest and joust
            and point this way and that and none know if thou be
            who thou sayst thou art or what others think thou
            be.

MARLOWE	And thou, Master Poley? Knowest thou who I am?
POLEY	Thy words tell me thou art my friend. More than that I do not wish to know.
MARLOWE	And thou, Friend Frizer, if friend thou art?
FRIZER	When friendship is dangerous wise friends keep their counsel.
MARLOWE	Wise words, Friend Frizer, so let us live dangerously and drink to friendship in all its masks!
FRIZER	*(uncertainly)* To friendship!
MARLOWE	Friend Poley, thou dost not drink.
POLEY	I drink, Friend Marlowe, but I do not drink to friendship.
MARLOWE	What dost thou drink to?
POLEY	That all traitors die.
MARLOWE	And thou, Master Skeres, drinkst to . . . ?
SKERES	To the death of heretics.
MARLOWE	Is there danger, Ingram Frizer, in our friendship? If so, where does it lie?
POLEY	If we knew where danger lay, there would be no danger.
SKERES	Danger lurks in words ill-advised.
MARLOWE	What words are ill-advised?
SKERES	Many words. Most ill are words that defy God and state.
MARLOWE	Such words are indeed ill-advised. I advise thee not to use them.
SKERES	And thou?
MARLOWE	I sir? I do not challenge state. And God is above all challenge.

SKERES   That is not thy reputation.

MARLOWE   What man is his reputation? A poor man may be
                more honourable than one of wealth.

SKERES   They say thou defamest the Bible.

MARLOWE   I only sometimes question what the Bible tells us.

SKERES   No honest man questions the Bible!

MARLOWE   No honest man does not! The stories the Bible tells
                us makes us question. Some who read might ask if
                Christ was a bastard or St John the Evangelist his
                bedfellow.

SKERES   Shame, sir, shame!

MARLOWE   But let us take the Bible at its word. What of those
                who see in priests and bishops more sinners than
                saints? Each man must see as well as he might.

POLEY   Dangerous words indeed.

Silence; they drink

MARLOWE   Robert Poley.

POLEY   Kit Marlowe?

MARLOWE   Thou asked about my next play.

POLEY   That I did.

MARLOWE   I did not answer honestly - or rather my answer was
                honest then but not so now.

SKERES   What mean'st thou?

MARLOWE   Whilst we were talking my next play came to mind.
                Wilt thou hear it?

POLEY   Gladly.

SKERES   What is it called?

MARLOWE   I do not yet know; all I can say is it is a tragedy.

POLEY   Then let us hear it.

MARLOWE   There are three friends whose word cannot be trusted. Let us call them Frizer, Poley and Skeres.

FRIZER   Good names, all three.

MARLOWE   There is a fourth friend, call him Kit, who stands apart. Kit is a dangerous man.

POLEY   How dangerous?

MARLOWE   He knows them for who they are - scoundrels all. They wear the mask of honesty but none is honest.

SKERES   No?

MARLOWE   He knows what they would hide.

POLEY   What do they hide?

FRIZER   They take from fools and give to whores?

MARLOWE   As do many men.

SKERES   They sell secrets to the highest bidder?

MARLOWE   A common trade.

POLEY   Then what?

MARLOWE   One spies for France and Spain. One has killed a man in the dark night. The third is loyal to the Scottish king.

POLEY   And which is which?

MARLOWE   Who knows? Perhaps none, perhaps all. It is but a play.

SKERES   How does it finish?

MARLOWE   In death of course.

FRIZER   Whose death?

MARLOWE   That I must decide. Which would please the crowd most? The Spanish spy? The murderer? The barbarian Scot?

FRIZER   Not Kit?

MARLOWE   Not Kit. He is the hero. He must survive.

POLEY   Wherein lies the tragedy?

MARLOWE   All three villains were once good men, till tempted by
              the world.

FRIZER   What temptations brought them low?

MARLOWE   Coin of the realm, women of the streets, a rich man's
              table. Perhaps all three.

POLEY   I like thy play.

SKERES   So do I.

FRIZER   I hold my judgement.

MARLOWE   The wisest among us.

POLEY   What is't called?

MARLOWE   I know not yet.

He drinks

              Mistress Bull!

SKERES   We have not finished what food and drink we have.

MARLOWE   I tire of talk and would to bed.

              Mistress Bull!

BULL appears

              We would have the reckoning. Ah, there, my friends,
              is the title of my play! The Reckoning - be it Mistress
              Bull's charge upon our purse or God's weighing of our
              soul.

POLEY   Or the hangman's rope round the condemned man's
              neck.

BULL   Talk not of such things, I beg you. Three shillings do
              you owe me.

FRIZER   Nine pence a man.

POLEY   Here's mine.

SKERES   And mine.

EDWIN enters and begins to gather the plates

MARLOWE   Where is the boy?

EDWIN   I will not send him.

FRIZER   Thy ninepence, Kit.

MARLOWE   No, Friend Frizer. My share is six pence. I only drank. Thou atest the lion's share.

FRIZER   I did not.

MARLOWE   By the grease on thy hands, I say thou didst.

FRIZER   And by the ale on thy doublet I say thou drankst my share. Ninepence, Master Kit.

MARLOWE   *(to EDWIN)* Where is the boy?

FRIZER   Nine pence, I say.

MARLOWE   The boy!

BULL   What want you with the boy, Master Marlowe?

FRIZER   Poley, Skeres, stand by me. Ninepence is all I ask.

POLEY   This quarrel is not mine.

SKERES   Nor mine

MARLOWE   I want the boy for nothing but to free him from that villain's grasp.

EDWIN   I am no villain!

MARLOWE   He suffers thy beating and abuse for thy pleasure. That is villainy.

FRIZER   Three pence more, Marlowe!

MARLOWE   Thy three pence be damned, Frizer.

BULL   Gentlemen, be calm.

MARLOWE   Where anger is righteous no man can be calm.

FRIZER   Come, what is three pence to one such as thee?

MARLOWE   One such as me?

FRIZER   A favourite of my master.

MARLOWE   Not much in favour in recent days. *(throws down six pence)* That is my debt. Now, the boy.

MARLOWE heads to the inner door, EDWIN pulls him back

EDWIN   The boy is mine.

MARLOWE   *(pulling out his dagger)* Lay not hands on me.

BULL   Keep the peace, I beseech you! Edwin, go fetch the boy!

EDWIN   *(pulling out his own dagger)* I will not.

FRIZER   *(pulling MARLOWE's doublet)* Thy share is ninepence.

Surprised, MARLOWE turns and by accident wounds FRIZER, who falls to his knees

MARLOWE   By Hades! What have I done?

EDWIN   *(wounding MARLOWE)* You shall not have him!

BULL   Gentlemen!!

MARLOWE   *(unaware he has been hit; kneeling, to FRIZER, who is in shock)* My friend, what ill fortune is this?

EDWIN   *(stabbing MARLOWE again)* The boy is mine!

BULL   Edwin! God's Blood, this is madness! Get thee hence! Be not discovered here!

EDWIN hurriedly exits. POLEY and SKERES are exchanging glances. FRIZER is groaning.

MARLOWE   *(standing)* A physician, Mistress Bull. My friend is
            wounded! Send for a physician!

            (becoming aware of his own wounds) Yet whose
            blood is this? My own? Didst thou, friend Frizer . . . ?
            Or was it . . . ?

POLEY   Thou hast killed him!

MARLOWE   Frizer? No, he lives!

FRIZER makes to rise but SKERES pushes him down

SKERES   Indeed, Robert Poley. This man I once called friend
            revealed his poignard and struck poor Ingram here..

MARLOWE   I raised my dagger against the man Edwin.

POLEY   What man Edwin? Where is he?

MARLOWE   Mistress Bull!

BULL   I know no man . . .

POLEY   *(stabbing MARLOWE)* Enough! Thou betrayed thy
            friend, some say thy country too.

MARLOWE   Aagh! Poley?

BULL   My masters! Peace, I beseech you!

SKERES   *(stabbing MARLOWE)* And all heard thee blaspheme
            against our Lord. Thus should all heretics die.

MARLOWE   Thou too, friend Skeres? Traitor? Heretic? Is Kit
            Marlowe thus damned?

            Ah, Gentlemen, you have heard my words but not my
            meaning. All I said was jest.

            And so I bring my fate upon myself. I fault you not.
            Like actors in my play you have been proud, bold,
            pleasant and resolute - then stabbed as occasion
            served. And so I die.

MARLOWE dies

BULL	What have you done? A man murdered in my tavern!
FRIZER	*(rising)* Ye fools. There dies the brightest star in England at your hand.
POLEY	Our hand? I think not, Ingram Frizer. 'Tis thou art wounded, not I. Mistress Bull, a physician, we beseech you!
SKERES	Mistress Bull, what didst thou see?
BULL	Good sir, remind me.
POLEY	Master Marlowe struck the first blow at Ingram Frizer here.
SKERES	Thou brought the reckoning. There was dispute. Masters Frizer and Marlowe quarreled. An unlucky accident.
FRIZER	I will not be sentenced for murder.
SKERES	Nor shalt thou be. Thy wound is witness of thy defence. Thou wilt be pardoned.
FRIZER	But it was thou, Robert Poley, that struck the fatal blow. And thou, Nicholas Skeres, struck too.
POLEY	Thine eyes deceived thee or thou wanderst in delirium, Ingram Frizer, to accuse me of murder.
SKERES	Or me.
POLEY	And Mistress Bull would not wish to swear to such deceit.
BULL	Indeed not, sir. I wish only to state the truth, whatever that might be.
SKERES	Will not several worthy gentlemen rejoice at Marlowe's passing? Sir Walter Raleigh, my Lord Burghley, the Earl of Essex, none of these have reason to love him, and thou, Robert Poley, and thou, Ingram Frizer, be known to all three gentlemen.

SKERES (cont)   Perhaps a word was spoken into a willing ear and gold passed into a waiting hand. Today the deed was done by a villain who ran from here as fast as thought. What thinkest thou of that story, Mistress Bull?

BULL   'Tis true, sir, I have heard of many quarrels and plots and Kit Marlowe - God take his soul -

SKERES   - Or the Devil -

BULL   - was oft careless of speech and ill-loved by many.

POLEY   I like better that he was stabbed by a serving-man, a rival in lewd lechery. By his own word he loved, did he not, tobacco and boys.

BULL   As you say, sir. My eyes deceived me, I thought I saw your hand and heard your speech, but that cannot be.

POLEY   Indeed not, Mistress Bull, my hands are free of blood - though if Kit Marlowe had been a traitor, I needs must kill him.

SKERES   As I would help any heretic die.

FRIZER   But he was our friend, Kit Marlowe.

POLEY   Our dear friend.

SKERES   And as our friend we shall mourn him with heavy tears.

FRIZER   Great tears of woe.

POLEY   As crocodiles do.

SEX/ VIOLENCE
E, C, H, K

CAST

BRENDA (bouncer)   DEREK   JACKSON   LAURA   OPHELIA   TOM
BOY (14 yrs old)

Outside a nightclub

DEREK	Quiet tonight.
BRENDA	Yeah.
DEREK	Who's on?
BRENDA	Managing?
DEREK	Console.
BRENDA	New girl. Slick Chick.
DEREK	Is she?
BRENDA	That's her name.
DEREK	Any good?
BRENDA	How the fuck would I know? I'm out here.
DEREK	If she's new on the scene, no-one's interested. No wonder business is bad tonight.
BRENDA	You do all right on other nights.
DEREK	Good set by a well-known spinner, I sell more. You get more. Everyone's happy.
BRENDA	Right.

TOM enters

DEREK	All right, mate?
TOM	All right.
DEREK	Need anything?

TOM eyes BRENDA; she conspicously looks away

TOM	What've you got?
DEREK	E, C, H, K.
TOM	You're a fucking pharmacy.
DEREK	Only the best.
TOM	Heard that before. Nah, you're all right.
DEREK	Sure? DJ tonight, you never heard anything like her grooves. Fucking fantastic. She'll take you up, just need that little extra to send you into fucking orbit. You won't come down for twenty-four hours. Only three quid for two Es. Get them now.
TOM	Maybe later.
DEREK	Might not be here later.
TOM	I'll take that chance.

BRENDA lets him in to the club

BRENDA	Great sales patter.
DEREK	You were no fucking use. You want your cut, get me the punters.
BRENDA	What do you want me to do? Push them up against the wall, throw you their wallet? Half of them don't carry cash any more.
DEREK	So I take phone.
BRENDA	Not worried about being traced?
DEREK	I get a burner every couple of days.
BRENDA	Legitimate business expense.
DEREK	Fucking right!
BRENDA	Why not resell? Hand them on?
DEREK	Who to?

BRENDA	One of your boys.
DEREK	What boys?
BRENDA	The boys who come round.
DEREK	Don't know what you're on about.
BRENDA	All right, all right. Just bants. Passing the time.

OPHELIA, JACKSON, LAURA enter

DEREK	Hey, babes!
OPHELIA	Hey.

They kiss intimately

DEREK	Bro.

Jackson raises a hand to high five, pulls it away before Derek can respond, does a little dance.

JACKSON	Hey, hey, hey, bro. How's it going?
DEREK	It's going good. Who's this?
OPHELIA	Laura. We met in the Duck. She's visiting family, doesn't know her way around.
DEREK	Welcome to Blitz, Laura. You'll have a great time. Fucking fantastic new spinner tonight, Quick Chick.
BRENDA	Slick Chick.
DEREK	Right, Slick Chick.
JACKSON	Quick and slick, quick and slick, that's me.
OPHELIA	Down, boy!
DEREK	Christ, you started early tonight, bro.
JACKSON	Yeah, yeah, thought you might have sold out.
DEREK	What're you celebrating?

JACKSON   Life, man! And the company of these beautiful,
               sexy, do-me-over girls.

DEREK   They're more likely to do me over, Jacko. Can I
               offer you anything, love? On the house.

LAURA   No, thanks, not tonight.

DEREK   Love, you don't know what you're fucking
               missing. Ask Feelie, she'll bring you up to speed -
               and if it's speed you need . . .

OPHELIA   Enough of the Feelie, my name's Ophelia!

DEREK   And I love to feel ya!

OPHELIA   Down, boy!

DEREK   *(pulls her hand to his crotch)* Only one thing'll
               make it go down now.

JACKSON   Any room for me in this party?

BRENDA   Oi! You lot, give it a break.

DEREK   Come on, Bren, just a bit of fun. Nothing you
               haven't seen before.

BRENDA   Usually at the end of the night.

DEREK   You're just jealous. Where's the girlfriend? You
               know I can dj you as well as she can.

               How about you, Laura? Like to party? I've got V
               for your boyfriend if he needs it. If he's not
               around I can always fill in, if you get my drift.

LAURA   I'm fine, thanks.

OPHELIA   You two go in. I want to spend a little time with
               this wanker.

DEREK   Only when you're not around, Phelia.

OPHELIA   See you inside.

JACKSON	Come on, girl, you're safe with me. I may be high as a kite but I'm sharp as a fox and I protect my friends like a tigress shields her cubs. *(snarls)*
LAURA	Ok.
JACKSON	Besides, I'm in the mood for bull tonight, not pussy.
DEREK	In your dreams, bro.

BRENDA opens the door and JACKSON and LAURA exit

DEREK	Give us space, will you, Bren?
BRENDA	I'll be inside.

BRENDA exits: DEREK and OPHELIA kiss

DEREK	I've missed you, babes. I'm as horny as a rabbit. Feel that. And let me . . .
	God, you're a prick tease. Help me out here before I explode.
OPHELIA	Can't, got to look after Laura.
DEREK	What the fuck for?
OPHELIA	I said I'd show her around.
DEREK	She looks a right drag.
OPHELIA	She's all right, a bit weird. One minute she's chatty, downing shots with the best of them. Next got a face like fucking thunder.
DEREK	So why let her hang around?
OPHELIA	Because she's buying all the drinks. Says she's celebrating but won't say what.
DEREK	So how come she's like she's at a funeral?
OPHELIA	Fuck knows. I offered her a hit.
DEREK	Giving, not selling, right?

OPHELIA   I'm not going to queer your pitch.

DEREK   Fucking right, you're not. No-one, not even my
                 girlfriend, sells around here without my approval.

OPHELIA   You're talking like a New York gangster.

DEREK   Just protecting the market. So she's some rich
                 uptight bitch who's latched on to you because
                 she's too frightened to go out on her own. Dump
                 her. Business is bad tonight. Five more minutes
                 and I'll be coming in.

OPHELIA   Come in now.

DEREK   Nah, I've got to see someone first.

OPHELIA   Who?

DEREK   Business, babe, business.

OPHELIA   "Don't worry your pretty little head, Phelia."
                 Sometimes you can be a right prick.

DEREK   My prick is all you need.

OPHELIA   Don't kid yourself, lover boy. When I've had
                 enough of your prick . . .

DEREK   You'll never have enough.

OPHELIA   . . . I'm moving on.

DEREK   No, babe. When I've had enough, you move on.
                 Until then we'll fuck each other crazy. Now fuck
                 off, I'll see you inside.

OPHELIA grabs hold of his crotch and squeezes.

                 Christ! What's that for?

OPHELIA   Just a reminder, you need this handful a lot more
                 than I do. Anything happens to it, I don't care. i
                 can always find another. You can't.

She squeezes harder

106

DEREK   Aagh! You fucking cunt!

OPHELIA   That's right. MY fucking cunt. I'm the one who decides what goes in it and when and how long for, and don't you forget it.

She releases her grip.

DEREK   That one's on me, bitch. Do it again and you'll regret it.

OPHELIA   Bitch? You don't know the half of it.

DEREK   Ok, Phelia, cool it. I'll see you inside. We'll dump Jackson and Lolita and have the night to ourselves. Even a little rough stuff if you're in the mood.

OPHELIA   Depends who's getting rough with who.

She gives him a long deep kiss then pulls away.

DEREK   Christ, Pheel, *(approvingly)* you are a bitch.

BRENDA opens the door as OPHELIA approaches, lets her in

BRENDA   Too cold out. I'm staying in.

DEREK   I'll be in shortly.

Alone, he adjusts his crotch, walks casually away to where he can't be seen from the club door. There, he looks around, pulls various small packets out of pockets, checks them and puts them back. He taps his foot purposefully.

BOY approaches nervously

DEREK   Where the fuck have you been?

BOY   I wasn't sure . . .

DEREK   Shut up. What've you got?

BOY   Here . . .

BOY hands DEREK an envelope. He turns his back and checks it, then turns back.

107

DEREK	How much is there?
BOY	Four fifty.
DEREK	How much should there be?
BOY	Five hundred.
DEREK	So where's the rest of it?
BOY	He didn't turn up. I didn't . . .
DEREK	Who didn't turn up?
BOY	Don't know his name. The Irish guy.
DEREK	Bloody Mick. So what did I tell you to do?
BOY	What?
DEREK	What did I fucking tell you to do if a punter doesn't show up?
BOY	F-f-find another?
DEREK	F-f-find another, make one of the regulars take it, stuff it up your arse and lift any cash you owe me from a Paki shop. Anything but don't fucking dare come back to me with less than the deal or I shall beat the fuck out of you, then fuck the shit out of you then fucking dump you in the fucking river, have you got that?
BOY	Yeah, Del, sorry. Won't happen again.
DEREK	You're fucking right it won't happen again. But you're in luck because I'm going to be good to you. You're new and I'll let you off that fifty. This time only. Next time - there won't be a next time. Got it?
BOY	Yeah, Del, got it.
DEREK	Even better, it's your lucky day and I'm going to do you a favour. Two favours in fact.
BOY	What?

DEREK	Here's your living expenses. Christ! Don't count it in the open like that. Anyone could see. Next, same shit, same price as before but ten packs instead of eight. Pay me for nine and the tenth's a bonus.
BOY	Who's the ninth for?
DEREK	That's up to you. Use your fucking initiative! Find new customers, only use your head. You don't want the feds after you. You know what happens to boys like you in prison, don't you? You really don't want it up your arse ten times a day, do you? And if you think you could get off by naming me, you'll be dead within the week. Got it?
BOY	Got it, Del, got it.
DEREK	Anything else?
BOY	No, Del. Can I go now?
DEREK	Where're you going?
BOY	Back to the room. I'm in the middle of a game.
DEREK	Got food?
BOY	Yeah.
DEREK	Warm enough?

BOY shrugs

DEREK	Anyone causing trouble? They're dead meat if they are.

BOY shakes his head

DEREK	See how I look after you? Stick with me and you'll get rich.
BOY	Can I go now?
DEREK	I said two favours. Here's the other. Open your mouth.

BOY   What?

DEREK   I said open your mouth.

BOY is reluctant. With one hand DEREK prises open his mouth and with the other pushes a pill in. BOY can't help but swallow.

DEREK   That'll help you win your game, see if it doesn't.
       Speed up your co-ordination.

BOY   What is it?

DEREK   That's my little secret. And if it doesn't win your
       game you'll have a woodie so hard you'll be
       whacking it all night long. Now fuck off . . .

BOY runs off

DEREK heads towards the door but it opens before he can get there. TOM comes out.

DEREK   All right, mate? Changed your mind?

TOM   Could be.

DEREK   What're you up for?

TOM   What've you got?

DEREK   E, C, H . . .

TOM   Sell to anyone, do you?

DEREK   Within reason.

TOM   Nice earner, is it?

DEREK   Don't know what you're talking about.

TOM   Dealing.

DEREK   Are you fed?

TOM shakes his head

       Do you want to buy or not?

TOM   Sure, I'll buy, but why should I buy from you?

DEREK   Coz I'm the only source around.

TOM   Not what I hear.

DEREK   What do you hear?

TOM   You've got a team working for you, I hear.
               Running. Selling.

DEREK   You heard wrong. Ok, mate, good talking to you.
               Have a nice life.

DEREK is going to open the door when JACKSON comes out.

JACKSON   *(over-friendly)* Hey, hey, hey, Del boy!

DEREK   Where's Bren?

JACKSON   Inside, doing her thing. And she's got a beautiful
               thing and . . .

DEREK   Get her to come out, will you?

TOM   I think she's busy.

DEREK   You, fuck off. I don't know who you are, but
               you're not welcome in this club. Jacko, get Bren
               out here. She can handle this piece of shit.

TOM   I don't think I'm the one who's shit.

DEREK   Jacko!

JACKSON   Del, Del, Del, we need to talk.

DEREK   Talk? What about? Everything ok with Phelia?

JACKSON   Talk about what's been going down, man.

DEREK   Nothing's going down apart from this shitbag on
               my case. Get Brenda out here, she'll sort him out,
               we'll enjoy the evening.

Door opens, BRENDA looks out

BRENDA   Everything ok?

TOM   We're good.

DEREK	Bren, come here a mo!
BRENDA	Don't think you need me.

BRENDA goes back inside

DEREK	What the fuck's going on? You two know each other?
TOM	Not before tonight.
JACKSON	We just met. That's the thing about clubs. You go to meet your mates, you go to drink, you go to get off your head, you go to get with someone horny, and sometimes . . .
DEREK	Shut the fuck up, Jacko, you're being a right arsehole tonight.
JACKSON	Arsehole, that's a good one. No, that's a sad one, that's a very sad one.

Door opens, OPHELIA comes out

DEREK	Phiel, let's go. I've had enough. This weirdo's coming on to me and Jacko's off his head.
OPHELIA	Not yet, Del. I want to get something straight first.
DEREK	What??
OPHELIA	Tell me about Taylor, Del.
DEREK	Who's Taylor?
OPHELIA	You know who Taylor is, don't you, Del? That boy that was always hanging around.
DEREK	What boy?
OPHELIA	You know the one I mean.
JACKSON	You know the one she means. I know the one she means. Tom knows the one she means. Everyone knows the one she means.

OPHELIA   Taylor, fourteen, mixed race, skinny.

JACKSON   My height. Good-looking but far too young.

TOM   Haven't seen him around lately, have you?

DEREK   What's this got to do with you?

OPHELIA   You haven't seen him, have you?

DEREK   I don't know. I don't remember. Didn't even
                 know his name.

OPHELIA   Oh, I think you did, Del boy. I always wondered
                 what you saw in him. Knew you always wanted it.
                 Didn't think you were queer.

DEREK   I'm not queer. He was just hanging around. Heard
                 I dealt, wanted to get in on the action. I told him
                 no way.

TOM   Did you, Del, did you really?

DEREK   What's it to you? Why don't you fuck off,
                 whoever you are, before I put the boot in.

JACKSON   That's not what we heard, not what we heard, is
                 it, Phelia?

DEREK   Who gives a fuck what you heard?

JACKSON   We heard he was running for you.

DEREK   You heard wrong.

OPHELIA   We heard right. I always wondered.

DEREK   Nothing to wonder about. And even if he was it
                 was none of your business. I don't worry about
                 how you get your money; don't you worry about
                 me.

OPHELIA   Oh, I'm not worried about you, but I would be
                 worried about Taylor. Wonder what happened to
                 him?

113

DEREK	I don't know. I don't care what happened to him.
TOM	I care what happened to him.
DEREK	Christ. Who the fuck are you?
TOM	He was scared out of his fucking wits. That's the first thing that happened to him.
JACKSON	Scared, Del, scared. If I was a kid, I'd be scared of you.
DEREK	He wasn't a kid.
TOM	He was fourteen.
DEREK	So?

TOM suddenly punches DEREK

DEREK	Christ!

TOM hits him again

TOM	Then he met up with a shitbag who offered to take care of him.
DEREK	Phelia! Jacko! Get this maniac off me.
OPHELIA	Nothing to do with me, Del. It's all on you.
DEREK	What is?
TOM	Taking care meant selling drugs.

He hits DEREK in a frenzy, shouting

> Living in a grotty room on pot noodles, freezing cold, scared to run away because you *(punches DEREK)*, you *(another punch)*, you *(punch)* told him you'd kill him if he did.

DEREK falls

DEREK	*(weakly)* I swear, I swear . . .

TOM kicks him

BRENDA has opened the door and is watching with LAURA

DEREK	Phiel, Jacko, you don't believe . . .
OPHELIA	How did he die, Derek?
DEREK	What?
OPHELIA	How did he die?
DEREK	What do you mean? I don't know, I don't know.
TOM	Someone gave him a fucking overdose.
JACKSON	Del, Del, Del, Del, Del.
DEREK	Who's telling you all this shit? It was just . . .
TOM	A fucking overdose.
	Do you know who he was, you bastard, you fucking shitfaced bastard not fit to live?
DEREK	I . . .
LAURA	He was my little brother. My sweet, beautiful, frightened little brother who ran away from home because he was bullied at school and ended up in this shithole of a town where the only person he knew was the local dealer . . .
DEREK	*(getting up slowly)* He came to me!
TOM	He came to you because the bastards who told him to run away gave him your phone number and said you would help him.
DEREK	I did help him!
OPHELIA	Did you fuck.
DEREK	You don't believe them, Phiel. You can't believe them.
OPHELIA	I've seen the pictures, Del. Just now, in the club. You should have sent him home.
DEREK	He'd run away from home. It wasn't my fault. I wanted to help him.

TOM	So what did you do?
DEREK	Who are you? What's this to do with you?
OPHELIA	He's Laura's boyfriend.
TOM	How did you help him?
DEREK	Let him run for me. Paid him well for it. He wanted to do it.
OPHELIA	Did he fuck.
TOM	You got him hooked, so he had to work for you.
DEREK	No, I didn't. I swear I didn't. Tell them, Phiel.
OPHELIA	Explains a lot, Del. Couldn't see how you made that much money just from this club. You had to be selling elsewhere.
DEREK	I didn't want you involved.
JACKSON	He was fourteen!
DEREK	I didn't know how old he was. He was just one in a chain. And I didn't O.D. him. Whatever it was he took it voluntarily.
TOM	You fucking gave it to him.
DEREK	It was his choice.
JACKSON	He was fucking fourteen! Fourteen! Four-fucking-teen! You gave class A to a fourteen-year-old!
TOM	Then you raped him.
DEREK	No, no, no!
OPHELIA	You fucking bastard.
TOM	You raped him.
DEREK	He was having a bad trip. I was comforting him. That was all.
LAURA	You fucking raped him.

116

DEREK   He . . . He wanted it, I swear. The drug was
               making him horny.

JACKSON   No-one's horny on a fucking overdose.

DEREK   He was. And I . . .

OPHELIA   You're always fucking horny. But not a boy . . .

JACKSON   He was fourteen!

DEREK   He wanted it!

TOM hits him; DEREK doesn't respond.

TOM   He didn't fucking want it. *(punch)* He didn't want
               the drugs. *(punch)* He didn't want you. *(punch)*
               He didn't want anything but to be home and you
               fucking O.D.'d him, you raped him and you left
               him and you carried on life as if nothing had
               happened. *(punch, punch, punch)*

DEREK falls

DEREK   He was ok when I left him! I swear!

LAURA   And now he's dead. It took us three weeks to find
               out where he was and two days to find out who
               you were. You took my little brother from me,
               from my Mum, you evil fucking bastard.

LAURA falls on DEREK and starts beating him. She is in tears.

DEREK   *(weakly)* Bren, get help.

BRENDA   I don't think they need help, do you guys?

TOM   None at all.

*As BRENDA watches LAURA and TOM stand then they, JACKSON and
OPHELIA start kicking and punching and spitting on DEREK who
moves briefly and then lies motionless. A siren can be heard.*

Eleven Short Plays

.

SEX / VIOLENCE
EVERYONE'S DREAM

CAST
DETECTIVE
FREDDIE BEACH, 40s
PETER OAKES at 17 and 28
JACK, 17

A police interview room with BEACH on one side, OAKES (28)
opposite and DETECTIVE in the middle. BEACH and OAKES (28) are
unaware of each other. JACK and OAKES (17) also on stage but not
in the police station.

DETECTIVE	*(pressing recorder)* Friday 24th March 2023, 9.10 am, Detective Robin Stanhope and Frederick Beach present.
	Mr Beach, please confirm your full name and age.
BEACH	Frederick Robert Beach, forty-six years old.
DETECTIVE	Do you confirm that you have not requested a lawyer to be present?
BEACH	I confirm.
DETECTIVE	And you understand that anything we record may be used in evidence against you.
BEACH	I understand.
DETECTIVE	Mr Beach, do you remember events on the evening of Saturday 9th February 2013?
BEACH	That's more than ten years ago.
DETECTIVE	Correct. Do you remember events that evening?
BEACH	What events?

DETECTIVE	Let me refresh your memory. That evening there was a concert, a gig, an event at the King's Hall, wasn't there?
BEACH	Probably.
DETECTIVE	The headlined performers were Everyone's Dream, weren't they?
BEACH	If you say so.
DETECTIVE	I have the promotional material here and the archived webpage here. Do you see them?
BEACH	I do.
DETECTIVE	Will you read the last line on the flyer?
BEACH	"Freddie Beach Promotions".
DETECTIVE	Do you confirm that you are the owner and sole director of Freddie Beach Promotions?
BEACH	I am.
DETECTIVE	Did you attend the concert that evening?
BEACH	I did, if I remember rightly. It was sold out.
DETECTIVE	We agree that was the case.
BEACH	Pity they broke up soon afterwards. They had great potential, but the singer . . .
DETECTIVE	What about the singer?
BEACH	Callum? Some talent, too much ego and not enough restraint.
DETECTIVE	Restraint?
BEACH	Couldn't keep off the cocaine.
DETECTIVE	Cocaine, ah, did you supply him?
BEACH	I did not. I have never supplied any of my acts with illegal substances of any description. That

didn't stop them obtaining them whenever they needed.

DETECTIVE   Did you, do you use cocaine or any other drugs?

BEACH   No comment.

DETECTIVE   The accusation here not is your use of drugs but I am curious to know if it affected your behaviour that evening.

BEACH   My alleged behaviour.

DETECTIVE   Your behaviour, alleged or otherwise. Did you use any illegal drugs that evening?

BEACH   No comment.

DETECTIVE pauses the recording machine

DETECTIVE   Help me out here. I'm trying to understand what happened . . .

BEACH   What you say happened.

DETECTIVE   . . . what happened. Drugs may be a mitigating factor.

BEACH   Mitigating for who?

DETECTIVE   Had you taken any drugs that evening?

BEACH   No comment.

DETECTIVE sighs and continues recording

DETECTIVE   At what time did the concert finish?

BEACH   I don't remember.

DETECTIVE   I have information that Everyone's Dream came off stage after their encore that evening at approximately 11.15pm.

BEACH   If you say so.

DETECTIVE   Where were you at that time?

BEACH	I was probably front of house talking to other promoters. I'd say get in touch with them to confirm but they've probably all moved on by now. Not many stay in this business for the long haul.
DETECTIVE	But you do.
BEACH	I've been lucky.
DETECTIVE	Where did you go afterwards?
BEACH	Afterwards?
DETECTIVE	After the concert, after the promoters had left.
BEACH	I don't remember.
DETECTIVE	Let me remind you. You walked out the front, round to the stage door.
BEACH	Possibly.
DETECTIVE	Why would you do that? Why not walk through the venue if you wanted to see your group?
BEACH	You never know who's at the back door. Sometimes your eye picks on . . .
DETECTIVE	Exactly, sometimes your eye picks on . . .
BEACH	People want to give you their demo tapes.
DETECTIVE	Tapes?
BEACH	A turn of phrase. Flash drive, whatever. People'll do anything to get noticed. Handing something to you in person is better than sending an email that might never get read. I'm more likely to listen to it.
DETECTIVE	Get any acts that way?
BEACH	One or two. Stanislav Shepherd - you won't have heard him yet but he's good - he's one.
DETECTIVE	And that's all they want?

BEACH	Who?
DETECTIVE	Backstage Johnnies - isn't that what they used to be called?
BEACH	New one on me.
DETECTIVE	Is that all they want, the people at the stage door, to give you flash drives?
BEACH	Some are fans. They just want selfies.
DETECTIVE	Everyone's Dream was popular, wasn't it?
BEACH	For a couple of years.
DETECTIVE	What was it about them?
BEACH	What is it about any pop star? The looks, the music, the moment, they all come together.
DETECTIVE	And Everyone's Dream had that?
BEACH	In spades.
DETECTIVE	Who were their biggest fans? Teenage, older, male, female? Straight, gay?
BEACH	Teenagers. Girls, young gays.
DETECTIVE	How young?
BEACH	What's this got to do with anything?
DETECTIVE	What was the age of the hangers-on, the fans, the groupies, whoever, waiting at the stage door to see their idols?
BEACH	I didn't hand out a questionnaire.
DETECTIVE	What age would you say?
BEACH	If they were younger than sixteen, they looked older and they shouldn't have been there.
DETECTIVE	More male or more female?
BEACH	I didn't take a census and you can't always tell.

DETECTIVE	Did you recognise anyone there?
BEACH	No.
DETECTIVE	Did any of them recognise you?
BEACH	Some of them will have. I was quite well known and popular until this blew up.
DETECTIVE	You can't blame us for this. We're just doing our job. Did any of them recognise you?
BEACH	I said, I'm sure some did.
DETECTIVE	Including Peter Oakes.
BEACH	Who?
DETECTIVE	Peter Oakes. For the record I am showing the suspect a picture of Peter Oakes.
BEACH	When was this taken?
DETECTIVE	I couldn't say.
BEACH	I don't recognise him.
DETECTIVE	Peter Oakes says that you spoke to him.
BEACH	That's possible. I speak to hundreds, thousands of people. You can't expect me to remember each one. I'm a people person. That's my job. That's how I get talent, it's how I sell talent, it's how I make my money.
DETECTIVE	Mr Oakes says that he did not approach you; you approached him.
BEACH	Don't know what you mean by approach. I often ask the fans what they thought of the concert. Feedback, you need it.
DETECTIVE	Mr Oakes says . . .

DETECTIVE turns his attention to OAKES (28)

DETECTIVE	Friday 24th March 2023, 10.15 am, Detective Robin Stanhope and Peter Oakes present.
	Mr Oakes, please confirm your full name and age.
OAKES (28)	Peter Oakes, twenty-eight.
DETECTIVE	Do you confirm that you have not requested a lawyer to be present?
OAKES (28)	Am I being charged?
DETECTIVE	No, you are here purely as a witness.
OAKES (28)	Will I be charged?
DETECTIVE	You will be not charged for any activity in relation to the accusation against Frederick Beach. Do you require a lawyer to be present? You have the right to change your mind.
OAKES (28)	No, don't need one.
DETECTIVE	So, tell me in your own words what happened on the evening of Saturday 9th February 2013.
OAKES (28)	I went to the Everyone's Dream concert at the King's Hall.
DETECTIVE	On your own?
OAKES (28)	No, with a mate.
DETECTIVE	What was his, her name?
OAKES (28)	Jack Something. Don't remember. We've lost touch.
DETECTIVE	Good concert?
OAKES (28)	Great.
DETECTIVE	You were a fan?
OAKES (28)	Massive.
DETECTIVE	Still?

OAKES (28)	Nah, you grow out of that stuff.
DETECTIVE	What was it about them?
OAKES (28)	Everything. The music, the moves, the guys. Can still see them. *(sings)* "You are the one, the only one."
DETECTIVE	I remember. Not my cup of tea.
OAKES (28)	Not mine now, but then . . .
DETECTIVE	After the concert.
OAKES (28)	Afterwards, we went round the back, see if we could see them. Selfies, that kind of stuff.
DETECTIVE	Many people there?
OAKES (28)	Dunno. Fifty or so?
DETECTIVE	Was there anyone you were particularly hoping to see?
OAKES (28)	Lead singer, Callum Macrievie.
DETECTIVE	Hoping to get off with himi?
OAKES (28)	In my dreams.
DETECTIVE	So you are gay.
OAKES (28)	Gay, queer, whatever, never denied it.
DETECTIVE	Did you get off with him?
OAKES (28)	With Callum Macrievie? For a while I thought I was going to . . .
DETECTIVE	You did? You thought he was going to walk out that door, up to you and say "Come back to my place".
OAKES (28)	No.
DETECTIVE	So what did you mean when you said you thought . . .

126

OAKES (28)	It was what that bastard Beach said to me.
DETECTIVE	What?
OAKES (28)	I don't remember exactly, something like
BEACH	Enjoy the show?
OAKES (17)	Loved it.
JACK	Fucking fantastic.
BEACH	Who's your favourite?
OAKES (17)	Callum.
JACK	I prefer Stu, more aggressive.
BEACH	Like to meet them?
OAKES (17)	Would I fuck!
JACK	Can we?
BEACH	I might be able to arrange it.
OAKES (17)	Now?
BEACH	Not tonight. Another night.
OAKES (17)	When?
BEACH	I'll sort something out. Hang around, can you?
JACK	Sure!
BEACH	I'm not sure about Stu. Callum's usually got more time. Let me talk to them. Hang around, will you?
OAKES (17)	You bet!
DETECTIVE	Then what happened?
OAKES (28)	He went inside.
DETECTIVE	Frederick Beach went in the stage door and you stayed outside?
OAKES (28)	Me and Jack, yes.

DETECTIVE	And you waited.
OAKES (28)	Yes.
DETECTIVE	How long?
OAKES (28)	Don't know. Half an hour, maybe.
DETECTIVE	Then what happened?
OAKES (28)	The group came out and everyone was screaming but the bodyguards hustled them away.
DETECTIVE	Was Frederick Beach there?
OAKES (28)	He came out just as they were leaving.
DETECTIVE	What did he say?
BEACH	Hi, lads.
OAKES (17)	Did you talk to them?
BEACH	I'll tell you about it in the car. Do you want a lift?
OAKES (17)	Do we, Jack?
BEACH	Sorry, it's a two-seater, only one of you.
OAKES (17)	*(to JACK)* What do you reckon?
JACK	*(to BEACH)* He's the one you fancy, is it?
BEACH	Might do. *(to OAKES)* How old are you?
OAKES (17)	Seventeen.
BEACH	Over the age of consent.
OAKES (17)	Yeah.
BEACH	I'm not going to force you. You fancy a ride in a Porsche, talk about the group, see what I can arrange, come with me. No skin off my nose if you don't.
OAKES (17)	What do you think?
JACK	Nothing to do with me. You're the one he fancies. If you fancy him . . .

128

DETECTIVE	Did you fancy him?
OAKES (28)	Nah! God, he was twice my age.
BEACH	Look, I'm Freddie Beach, I'm not stupid. No harm's going to come to you. I've got a reputation to keep up.
OAKES (17)	Yeah, I'll come.
DETECTIVE	So then what happens?
OAKES (28)	I get into his car and we go for a drive.
BEACH	You ever been in a Porsche before?
OAKES (17)	No.
BEACH	I'll show you what it can do.
DETECTIVE	So you admit you went with him voluntarily.
OAKES (28)	Yeah, but I wouldn't if I'd known.
DETECTIVE	Where did you go?
OAKES (28)	Around, ended up on
BEACH	Old Man's Hill. Good view from here.
OAKES (17)	Yeah.
DETECTIVE	So you're up on Old Man's Hill.
OAKES (28)	Yeah.
DETECTIVE	And what happens?
BEACH	Why not undo your seatbelt? Make yourself comfortable.
OAKES (17)	Ok.
BEACH	And your trouser belt, if you like.
OAKES (17)	Are you coming on to me?
BEACH	Only if you want it.

OAKES (17)	I dunno.
BEACH	Have you had much sex?
OAKES (17)	Some.
BEACH	Seventeen. Got a hard-on all the time, don't you?
OAKES (17)	More or less.
BEACH	Got to deal with it somehow.
OAKES (28)	He comes on to me.
DETECTIVE	How?
BEACH	Can I touch it?
OAKES (17)	Ok *(gasps)*
BEACH	Like the way I do it?
OAKES (17)	Oh, yeah, man.
OAKES (28)	Before I know it, he's leaning over and kissing me. God, it was disgusting; I can still smell his breath.
DETECTIVE	Is that all?
OAKES (28)	Nah, he's got my hand on my . . . down there.
DETECTIVE	What did you do?
OAKES (28)	I tried to push him off.
OAKES (17)	*(breathing heavily)* Yeah. Oh, that's good.
BEACH	Do you want put your hand there?
OAKES (17)	*(hesitating)* Okay.

BEACH breathes heavily.

DETECTIVE	Did you?
OAKES (28)	Did you what?
DETECTIVE	Push him off.
OAKES (28)	I tried, but he was bigger than me.

DETECTIVE   Tell me more.

OAKES (17)   Yeah, yeah. Fuck, your mouth, that's so good . . .

OAKES (28)   Must I?

DETECTIVE   The more details you give, the more likely it is we can charge him.

OAKES (28)   All I want to say is he forced me to perform an oral sexual act on him.

DETECTIVE   And you resisted?

BEACH   Will you go down on me?

OAKES (17)   I . . . Ok

BEACH   *(breathing heavily)* Take it easy . . .

OAKES (28)   You bet I resisted, but he pushed my head down, nearly choked me. I was in tears.

BEACH has an orgasm

BEACH   Fuck, you really know what you're doing.

OAKES (17)   Was I ok?

BEACH   Oh, yes. Your turn.

DETECTIVE   Then what happened?

OAKES (28)   When?

DETECTVE   After he, you, finished . . .

OAKES (17) has an orgasm

OAKES (28)   I couldn't finish. I was disgusted. He took me home.

DETECTIVE   That was it? He didn't threaten you?

OAKES (28)   Yeah, he did. Told me not to tell anyone. It was my word against his and he knew a lot of powerful people.

BEACH	I'd better get you home. Will there be any problems?
OAKES (17)	Nah, I'm staying over with Jack. What about . . .
BEACH	What about?
OAKES (17)	What about Callum?
BEACH	I'll be honest with you - I don't think it's going to happen. Wouldn't be good for either of you.
OAKES (17)	Right.
BEACH	Disappointed?
OAKES (17)	Kind of.
BEACH	Mad at me?
OAKES (17)	Dunno. Nah.
DETECTIVE	And did he drive you home?
OAKES (28)	Yeah, but . . .
DETECTIVE	But what . . . ?
BEACH	Here, take this.
OAKES (17)	What? What's it for?
BEACH	To make up for not meeting Callum. Just don't tell anyone, ok?
DETECTIVE	What?
OAKES (28)	He gave me two hundred quid.
DETECTIVE	What for?
OAKES (28)	To keep my mouth shut.
JACK	Hey, bro, I was getting worried.
OAKES (17)	Nothing to worry about. Went for a drive, that's all.
JACK	That's all?

OAKES (17)	Yeah, well, he took a load off.
JACK	What do you mean? *(laughs)* Seriously?
OAKES (17)	And I did the same for him.
JACK	Yeuch!
OAKES (17)	It wasn't that bad. And he gave me two hundred quid.
JACK	You're joking!
OAKES (17)	Nah, look.
JACK	Fuck me!
OAKES (17)	Take half, but don't tell anyone.
JACK	Why're you giving it to me?
OAKES (17)	Coz you lost out.
JACK	Man, you are a true friend.
DETECTIVE	Why didn't you go to the police?
OAKES (28)	I was scared. Wouldn't you be? A kid that age. Christ, I'd only just worked out I was gay. He's Freddie Beach. Who would people believe, him or me?
DETECTIVE	So why did you go back?
OAKES (28)	What?
DETECTIVE	In your statement, you said you went back three times. Why?
OAKES (28)	He made me.
BEACH	Thought I'd find you here.
OAKES (17)	Been looking for me?
DETECTIVE	How did he make you go back?
OAKES (28)	Said he'd tell my Mum, tell everyone at school.

BEACH   Thought you might like another ride in the
                 Porsche.

OAKES (28)   He said he knew some really heavy people, could
                 make my life a misery.

OAKES (17)   Same deal as before?

BEACH   Yeah. Well?

OAKES (17)   All right.

BEACH   Nobody's forcing you.

OAKES (17)   I'll come.

BEACH   Good lad.

DETECTIVE   Same thing happen? He forced oral sex on you?

OAKES (28)   Yeah.

DETECTIVE   Anything else?

OAKES (28)   Does it make a difference?

DETECTIVE   We'll come back to that.

BEACH   You enjoy it, don't you?

OAKES (17)   Yeah!

BEACH   Got a boyfriend?

OAKES (17)   No.

BEACH   Girlfriend?

OAKES (17)   No way.

BEACH   That boy, Jack?

OAKES (17)   Just good mates. You got a boyfriend?

BEACH   Not at the moment. Go back?

OAKES (17)   Can we hang around here a little? I like the night
                 sky.

BEACH   Sure.

DETECTIVE	Anything different about that second time?
OAKES (28)	It was worse.
DETECTIVE	How worse?
OAKES (28)	I knew what was coming. I didn't want it. His smell . . .
DETECTIVE	And you still didn't tell anyone.
OAKES (28)	No.
DETECTIVE	That's what makes this job so difficult. Young people, children, get abused. Horrific situations but nobody comes forward and perverts get away with it.
OAKES (28)	But I came forward.
DETECTIVE	Ten years later. You said there was a third time.
BEACH	Go a ride up the coast?
OAKES (17)	Can't get enough of me, can you?
BEACH	Let's just say you've taken my fancy.
OAKES (17)	All right, then.
BEACH	No hesitation this time?
OAKES (17)	Nah. I trust you.
DETECTIVE	What happened the third time?
OAKES (28)	He tried to rape me.
BEACH	I'd love to fuck you.
OAKES (17)	I've never . . .
BEACH	Fancy the idea?
OAKES (17)	Yeah, but . . .
BEACH	But not now, or not with me.
OAKES (17)	Right.

BEACH	Can't say I'm not disappointed. But it's your choice.
DETECTIVE	He tried?
OAKES (28)	Fucking right, he tried. I had to fight him off.
DETECTIVE	And that was it?
OAKES (28)	That was it. He saw I was serious. Took me back. Never saw him again.
BEACH	Free this afternoon? Go anywhere you want to go.
OAKES (17)	Uh, Freddie . . .
BEACH	Yeah?
OAKES (17)	Do you mind?
BEACH	Mind?
OAKES (17)	If I don't.
BEACH	Another day?
OAKES (17)	Nah, it's . . . I've met someone. I want to . . .
BEACH	I get it. Has he got a Porsche? Only kidding. Good on you, lad, hope it works out. Well, I'll miss you.
OAKES (17)	Thanks for everything.
BEACH	Get in touch if you want to meet up again. Freddie Beach Promotions'll be around for a while.
DETECTIVE	What impact did the experience have on you?
OAKES (28)	It made me . . . , it made me feel disgusted with myself. Going back and letting him do it to me again. At times I wanted to kill myself. It's been a nightmare.
DETECTIVE	And you didn't see a therapist or a doctor or anyone about it? It would be evidence of impact.

OAKES (28)   No, I was too scared. Does that mean you can't . . . ?

DETECTIVE   With your statement, we'll pursue charges. With luck it'll stick. Thank you for your time. We'll be in touch. I'll show you out.

OAKES (28)   How much do you think I'll get?

DETECTIVE   What?

OAKES (28)   There's compensation, isn't there, even after all this time? I read somewhere up to forty grand.

DETECTIVE   You've a long way to get to that point, son, but if your story's straight, I'll see what we can do.

OAKES (28)   Do. The sooner that bastard's locked up, the better for everyone.

NOH

THE TRAGIC LOVE OF TWO ENEMIES

adapted from the story by Ihara Saikaku (1642-1693)

CAST

NARRATOR(S)

SENPATJI   WIFE/MOTHER   SHYNOSUKE

ACTORS playing all other roles

MUSICIAN(S)

The NARRATOR(S) is/are the only speaker(s)
SOUND cues are only suggestions

All actors are onstage at all time, coming forward as necessary and putting on character masks when appropriate. All words are spoken by the NARRATOR(S)

SOUND	*pleasant*
NARRATOR	In Etjigo Province
	Lord Jibudayu rules
SOUND	*serious*

JIBUDAYU comes forward

summons his Chief Minister,

CHIEF MINISTER comes forward

commands him

to have the courtier Shingokei

SHINGOKEI is seen in traditional pose

killed.

CHIEF MINISTER reacts with shock and then obedience

JIBADAYU and SHINGOKEI retire

SOUND	*thoughtful*

The Chief Minister ponders

SOUND   *lighter beat*

SENPATJI comes forward, young and full of life

                    and beckons young Senpatji.

CHIEF MINISTER orders SENPATJI to kill SHINGOKEI; SENPATJI is shocked and appears to refuse

                    "If the order comes from my Lord,"

                    Senpatji says,

                    "I must hear it from his lips".

SOUND   *serious*

JIBUDAYU comes forward; CHIEF MINISTER bows, SENPATJI prostrates himself

JIBUDAYU commands SENPATJI and he acknowledges the order

JIBUDAYU and CHIEF MINISTER retire; SENPATJI remains on one side of the stage

SOUND   *light, family*

SHINGOKEI and his WIFE come forward

                    Shingokei has a young wife.

                    He is proud and she is happy.

SOUND   *threatening beat*

SENPATJI strides to the (non-existent) door and enters

                    "I have come to kill you,"

                    Senpatji says

The WIFE is frightened. SHINGOKEI draws his sword

SENPATJI holds up his hand

                    "It is my Lord's command."

SHINGOKEI is surprised

SOUND   *reflecting the words and events below*

"No!" says the wife.

The WIFE throws herself at SENPATJI's feet

"It is my Lord's command," says Senpatji.

The WIFE begs

"It is my Lord's command!"

The WIFE places herself between them, prepares to die; SHINGOKEI pushes his WIFE away

"You are with child,"

Shingokei says.

WIFE crumples, looks on as SHINGOKEI drops his sword, bares his breast

SENPATJI looks at him and his WIFE, hesitates; courage returns and he kills SHINGOKEI

SOUND   portrays WIFE's grief

CHIEF MINISTER comes forward

The wife and unborn child are exiled.

SOUND   sad

WIFE retires

CHIEF MINISTER turns to SENPATJI, throws him a pouch of money

His work done,

Senpatji also must leave the court.

CHIEF MINISTER retires

SENPATJI retires, unhappy

SOUND   heavy

The woman wanders far, far away,

begs for food,

141

	begs for work,
	gives birth,
SOUND	*a crying baby*
	walks on and on
	until in a far province
	she makes a poor home
	for herself and her son,
	Shynosuke.

SHYNOSUKE comes forward

	Shynosuke grows into a handsome youth,
	kind and caring.

WIFE (now MOTHER) and SHYNOSUKE at one side of the stage

SOUND	*walking*

SENPATJI comes forward

	Senpatji too wanders,
	lives the life of a samurai.
SOUND	*fighting, singing*
	He grows older, wiser,
	but is still strong.
SOUND	*walking*
	One day he comes
	to a house at the edge of a town
SOUND	*a flute*
	and hears sweet music.
	He pushes open the door
	Mother plays her flute,

               her son reads,

               hears a sound,

               looks up,

               sees Senpatji

               and smiles.

SOUND   *flute music stops*

               Shenpatji has never seen

               such a handsome youth.

               Shynosuke has never seen

               such a handsome man.

               The mother hesitates

               then bids the stranger welcome

SENPATJI enters the house; MOTHER and SHYNOSUKE prepare to wait on him

               but they cannot feed him.

               Senpatji has food

               and invites them to join him.

SOUND   *uncertain*

               Shingokei's wife does not know his murderer.

               Senpatji does not know the widow.

               Shynosuke does not know his future.

SOUND   *pleasant*

               Senpatji is weary of wandering.

               The mother is weary of caring for her son.

               Shynosuke is ready to be a man.

               There is a hut nearby.

It is empty,

the mother says.

| SOUND | *anticipation* |

The boy's eyes plead.

The mother bows.

Senpatji stays.

| SOUND | *time passing* |

Time passes.

Senpatji respects the mother.

The mother honours Senpatji.

Senpatji teaches the son.

The son honours Senpatji.

Man and youth become intimate.

Life is good for all.

| SOUND | *gradually darkening mood* |

One night Senpatji talks of his youth

in Etjigo province.

The Mother listens,

remembers,

relives

the death of her husband.

SHYNOSUKE is studying; SENPATJI does not see the horror as the MOTHER remembers

| SOUND | *appropriate to what follows* |

The next day

Senpatji goes to the market.

The Mother tells the son

Senpatji killed his father.

"I pleaded for his life,"

she says,

but it was his master's command.

She begged Senpatji to kill her

but she was with child.

Shynosuke's father bared his breast

and died an honourable death.

Mother and child were exiled.

SOUND   *climax*

Now, the mother says,

Shynosuke must kill

his father's murderer.

His ghost, unavenged, demands it.

His widow, unavenged, demands it.

His honour, as yet unblemished, demands it.

SOUND   *strong emotion*

Shynosuke protests

he cannot kill his lover.

His mother is adamant.

Honour demands

Shynosuke must kill Senpatji.

SHYNOSUKE is in torment

"Avenge your father!"

"Are you a coward?"

"Has your love made you weak?"

"If you do not kill him,

I, a weak woman, will do so"

The MOTHER takes a dagger, makes to leave; SHYNOSUKE stops her

Shynosuke will do his duty.

It breaks his heart.

SHYNOSUKE takes the dagger; SENPATJI approaches, the MOTHER retreats but eavesdrops

SHYNOSUKE and SENPATJI embrace

Shynosuke reveals himself to Senpatji,

tells him he must kill him.

SENPATJI hangs his head in sorrow then bares his breast

As the son of a noble,

Shynosuke must act nobly,

take Senpatji's sword

to avenge his father.

Senpatji's life has no value.

Shynosuke hesitates.

How can he kill

the man who brought happiness to his home?

"Avenge your father!"

Senpatji says,

"or lose your honour."

They face each other,

the older man who is ready to die,

the younger man who must kill him,

their happiness now at an end.

SOUND   *rising tension*

Senpatji bares his breast.

Shynosuke raises his sword.

The MOTHER rushes in, falls to her knees between them.

"Wait!"

 the Mother cries.

"You are both noble."

She tells Senpatji

he must die.

She tells Shynosuke

he must kill his lover.

But first

they must have one last night

of love

together.

Tomorrow the deed must be done.

SOUND reflects the coming of night then celebration

The MOTHER brings in food and wine

SENPATJI and SHYNOSUKE eat, drink and embrace

Dawn comes.

Shynosuke takes his sword,

plunges it

into Senpatji's back

through his lover's body

until it pierces

his own heart.

They lie still in the early morning light.

SOUND   *as appropriate*

The Mother wakes,

calls her son to his duty

but hears no reply.

She enters their chamber.

The MOTHER wails

Never has the Mother seen

such nobility.

Never has the Mother seen

such love.

Never will the Mother see

such things again.

With a knife the MOTHER cuts her own throat and falls over the bodies.

GET A LICENCE!

CAST

LECTURER   ANNOUNCER   ACTORS
the number of Actors is determined by the company

*population statistics taken from
https://www.worldometers.info/world-population/world-population-by-year/*

sea level rise from Wikipedia

Amazon loss from https://sentientmedia.org/amazon-deforestation/

other figures from reliable internet sources

Either the scene begins with a short film demonstrating with clear visuals and minimal commentary the rapid rise in global human population over the last ten thousand years and its implications for the planet and people in general (loss of wildlife habitat and natural resources, global warming, starvation, mass migration etc) or the film is a silent backdrop throughout the performance without being so obtrusive that it detracts from the argument.

LECTURER	In the beginning . . .
ACTOR	The beginning of what?
LECTURER	Whatever you like. The universe, the world, this play . . .
ACTOR	Play?
LECTURER	Play, event, scenario, happening . . . whatever you want to call it. In the beginning there was, there were . . .
ACTOR	What?
ANNOUNCER	*(almost sotto voce)* Two thousand years ago, one hundred and seventy million.
LECTURER	People.

ACTOR	That isn't a beginning.
LECTURER	Homo sapiens. There was a point at which homo sapiens evolved from homo heidelbergensis . . .
ACTOR	Homo what?
LECTURER	At some point in the last three hundred thousand years ago, homo sapiens, human beings as we know ourselves today, became, as far as we can tell, the most intelligent and self-aware animals on the planet.
ACTOR	Is that where we begin?
LECTURER	Yes.
ACTOR	The beginning of what?
LECTURER	What are the characteristics of homo sapiens?
ANNOUNCER	*(slightly louder)* One thousand years ago, two hundred and seventy-five million.
ACTOR	There are a lot of us about.
ACTOR	Do we have to use "homo"?
LECTURER	It's a scientific term, referring to a species, not a sexual orientation.
ACTOR	If you insist.
LECTURER	I do. So what are the characteristics of homo sapiens?
ACTOR	We walk upright.
ACTOR	We use tools.
ACTOR	We have language.
ACTOR	We are self-aware.
LECTURER	Good to see you've done your homework. What else?

ANNOUNCER	*(each intervention slightly louder than the last)* Five hundred years ago, four hundred and fifty million.
ACTOR	What do you want?
ACTOR	We're intelligent.
LECTURER	Define intelligence.
ACTOR	The ability to acquire and apply knowledge and skills.
LECTURER	Such as?
ACTOR	Driving.
ACTOR	Engineering
ACTOR	Cooking.
ACTOR	Making love.
ACTOR	Isn't that instinct?
ANNOUNCER	Two hundred years ago, one billion!
LECTURER	Compare the predictable coupling of animals and birds with the inventiveness of the Kama Sutra.
ACTOR	If only I had the opportunity to try every position in that work . . .
LECTURER	What other skills?
ACTOR	Writing.
ACTOR	Making things.
ACTOR	Weapons.
ACTOR	The internet.
ACTOR	Art.
ACTOR	Music.

LECTURER	And so on. But homo sapiens began with little knowledge and much consumption, excretion and copulation.
ANNOUNCER	One hundred years ago, two billion!!
ACTOR	Otherwise known as eating and drinking, pissing and shitting, and fucking.
ACTOR	There are children present!
ACTOR	Will we ever get to the point?
ACTOR	What is the point?
LECTURER	Let's focus on sex. Why do animals copulate? That's a trick question, by the way.
ACTOR	How?
LECTURER	Because "why" has two meanings - either "what was the cause" or "what is the intended result". "Why" can cover past or future and sometimes both. Animals copulate because . . .
ANNOUNCER	Nineteen sixty, three billion!!!
ACTOR	. . . their hormones or genes or whatever tell them to.
LECTURER	The past, the cause.
ACTOR	Or to produce offspring.
LECTURER	The future, the hoped for result. Bravo!
ACTOR	You can be condescending.
LECTURER	That's animals. We're animals too but with a few extra features. Why do we have sexual intercourse?
ACTOR	For pleasure.
ACTOR	To have children.
ACTOR	Because some of us are forced to.

LECTURER	Leave that unpleasant and far too common last statement to one side along with the obvious pleasure. Many of us have intercourse - or use test tubes and spatulas - in order to reproduce.
ACTOR	Just say "make babies".
ACTOR	"have children".
LECTURER	Have children.
ANNOUNCER	Nineteen seventy-four, four billion!!! !
ACTOR	Not always. Sometimes it's a mistake - the condom bursts, the pill doesn't work, the woman has no choice.
LECTURER	Thank you. I was getting to that point. So why are there so many children today?
ACTOR	Because they don't die.
LECTURER	Because . . .
ACTOR	There are no predators.
ACTOR	Far less disease than there used to be.
ACTOR	People want them.
ACTOR	They're proof of wealth.
ACTOR	Or poverty.
ACTOR	Of love.
LECTURER	And lack of intelligence.
ANNOUNCER	Nineteen eighty-seven, five billion!!!!!
ACTOR	What has intelligence got to do with it?
LECTURER	Forget children for a while. Think about what intelligence should do, particularly when confronted with a problem.
ACTOR	A child is a problem?

LECTURER   One isn't. A hundred million is. But I said, put children to one side.

ACTOR   So tell us about intelligence.

ACTOR   Our level of which distinguishes us from the animals.

LECTURER   True intelligence would identify problems and find solutions. It would distinguish between causes and consequences and between short- and long-term goals. But the human brain doesn't do any of these things. We always seek short-term gain and fail to understand long-term consequences.

ACTOR   I don't get it.

LECTURER   Every human invention creates as many or more problems as it solves.

ACTOR   Such as?

LECTURER   Fossil fuels. For two hundred years coal and oil gave us heat, warmth and cooking. Only now do we see the damage we have done to our climate.

ANNOUNCER   As a result of global warming, in the last hundred years sea-levels have risen by twenty centimetres.

LECTURER   Or the internet. It's brought everyone closer together and unleashed an unstoppable torrent of hatred and lies. Artificial Intelligence? We have no idea what destruction it will cause but our track record of creating inventions we don't understand and predicting the future is anything but good.

ACTOR   I don't see what that has to do with children.

LECTURER   Focusing on children who are wanted, why are they brought into the world?

154

ANNOUNCER   Nineteen ninety-nine, six billion!!! !

ACTOR   To give the parents pleasure.

ACTOR   Comfort in old age.

ACTOR   To conquer loneliness.

ACTOR   The maternal . . .

ACTOR   . . . paternal . . .

ACTOR   . . . parental . . .

ACTOR   . . . instinct.

LECTURER   Each of these reasons apart from the last is
              purely selfish. I want a child and so I will have
              one. My life has no meaning without a child and
              so I will create one. All my friends have children
              and so should I. God tells me to. Society tells me
              to. My genes and hormones tell me I must
              become a parent. If those are the causes, what
              are the consequences?

ACTOR   Of being a parent?

ANNOUNCER   TWO THOUSAND AND ELEVEN, SEVEN BILLION!!

LECTURER   Of creating a child.

ACTOR   Pleasure.

ACTOR   Responsibility.

ACTOR   Headache.

ACTOR   Heartache.

ACTOR   Cost.

ACTOR   Love.

ACTOR   Laughter.

ACTOR   Everything. There can be no greater joy or,
              sometimes, pain.

155

LECTURER	Joy and pain for who?
ACTOR	The parent, the parents.
LECTURER	And for the rest of us? For the environment? For the planet? For the future? What benefit and what damage does a child bring?
ANNOUNCER	TWO THOUSAND AND TWENTY-THREE, EIGHT BILLION!!
ACTOR	I don't understand.
LECTURER	That is the problem. Few people do.
ACTOR	What?
LECTURER	Few people understand the impact their children have on other people's lives, including their siblings.
ACTOR	Impact on other people's lives?
ACTOR	On a brother or sister?
LECTURER	The impact of your child's existence on my life.
ACTOR	None at all. How could it, if your lives never cross?
LECTURER	What impact do a thousand, a million, children have? Your child has a share in it.
ACTOR	Tell me.
LECTURER	They all need to be fed, to be housed, to be clothed.
ACTOR	Of course.
LECTURER	They want to be entertained. They want to learn. They want presents and toys and footballs and playstations and smartphones and . . .
ACTOR	So?

LECTURER	So every child, like every adult, is competing for an ever-diminishing supply of resources on a planet that is rapidly heating and where shelter and nourishment is increasingly difficult to find.
ACTOR	So we have to recycle and stop climate change.
ANNOUNCER	IN TWENTY THIRTY-SEVEN THERE WILL BE NINE BILLION PEOPLE ON A PLANET THAT CAN BARELY SUPPORT . . .
LECTURER	Are you doing your bit?
ACTOR	As much as I can.
LECTURER	So you buy nothing new because everything new depletes resources and even if everything is recycled energy is required in manufacture.
ACTOR	Well . . .
LECTURER	And you no longer travel anywhere, even by public transport because even electrical vehicles use power that is frequently generated by fossil fuel.
ACTOR	That's impossible.
ACTOR	We have to live.
ACTOR	Sometimes take a holiday.
ACTOR	Get out of the house, the flat, the whatever . . .
LECTURER	And most of all, you've decided not to have children because you know that whatever pleasure that child might give you, as it grows and long after you are dead it will continue to compete with all the other children that are born each year for rapidly disappearing natural resources.
ACTOR	It's my right to have a child.
ACTOR	More than one.

157

ACTOR   As many as I want.

ACTOR   As long as I can look after them.

ACTOR   And if I can't feed them, the state will.

LECTURER   Will it? Who is the state? You? You? You? You?

ACTOR   Who will look after us when we get ill?

ACTOR   Who will look after you *(LECTURER)* when you get ill?

LECTURER   So we breed more children today to look after us tomorrow and the spiral continues until . . .

ACTOR   Something will sort itself out.

ACTOR   Science.

ACTOR   Technology

ANNOUNCER *(normal voice)* The Jevons Paradox.

ACTOR   Human ingenuity. Look at all the things we've invented. See how we've made so many things more efficient.

ANNOUNCER *(slightly louder)* The nineteenth century political economist William Jevons . . .

ACTOR   We need far fewer resources for many things we use.

ANNOUNCER *(louder)* . . . demonstrated that the more efficiently we manufacture an object, the more resources it uses up.

ACTOR   That doesn't make sense.

LECTURER   If you use fewer resources to manufacture something - say a car - that makes it cheaper. If you make cars cheaper, more people buy one. The more people that buy a car the more resources are used up, even if each individual car uses far fewer resources than before.

ANNOUNCER	*(emphatic)* The cheaper things are, the more people buy them. The more people buy cheap goods, the more resources are depleted.
ACTOR	Are you listening, Primark?
ACTOR	More important, are the people who buy at Primark . . .
ACTOR	. . . or any company that sells cheap goods . . .
ACTOR	. . . or sells cheap flights, . . .
ACTOR	. . . accelerating the destruction of the planet,
ACTOR	are they listening?
ANNOUNCER	*(insistent)* The Jevons Paradox!
ACTOR	So we're all doomed.
LECTURER	We've been doomed since we first became homo sapiens. We developed the right amount of intelligence both to evolve and destroy us.
ACTOR	That's even more cheerful.
LECTURER	We are blissfully unaware that the children we create to bring us comfort and pleasure are the seeds of their own destruction as we all demand more and more from the planet and the environment.
ANNOUNCER	The Amazon has lost nearly twenty percent of its original size.
LECTURER	Parenthood is essentially selfish, always intended to gratify the parent not the infant.
ACTOR	Rubbish!
ACTOR	You cannot be selfish and bring up a child.
LECTURER	You create a child precisely because you are selfish. It is either a deliberate act of conception

LECTURER (cont)	or a failure to take precautions or to abort the bundle of cells before it becomes human.
ACTOR	You have a very cynical view of people's motives.
LECTURER	How many potential parents think to ask a child before it is conceived whether it wants to exist? You thrust existence on it and force it to fight survive and prosper.
ACTOR	Don't you want to survive?
LECTURER	We all do once we are forced into existence, but the rational choice - the impossible and paradoxical choice - might be to refuse to be born.
ACTOR	Ashton Kutcher did that in *The Butterfly Effect*.
ACTOR	Thanks for that spoiler!
ACTOR	So what's your solution?
ACTOR	To life, the universe and everything?
ACTOR	Suicide?
LECTURER	Not rational. I'm here and I'm selfish and I'll stay as long as I want to and can, but I won't impose my genes on the next generation.
ACTOR	If the ultimate cause of all our problems is the population explosion, what is the solution?
ACTOR	Better education?
ACTOR	Penalties for pregnancy?
LECTURER	You're getting close. What do you need to drive a car?
ACTOR	A licence.
LECTURER	To own a gun?
ACTOR	A licence.
LECTURER	To fly a plane?

ACTOR   A licence.

LECTURER   To sell alcohol?

ACTOR   A licence.

LECTURER   To create a child?

ACTOR   A stiff dick.

ACTOR   Do you have to use that language?

ACTOR   An erect penis.

ACTOR   And an egg.

LECTURER   Exactly. A minute or more to spurt into a womb
              or a test-tube and the result lasts a lifetime. Not
              just the life of the child but of everyone around
              it. A casual act committed in love or for money or
              with passion or through inattention or in violence
              has consequences that ripple through time for
              generation after generation as . . .

ANNOUNCER   . . . every minute of every day two hundred and
              fifty-three babies are born - a hundred and thirty-
              three million a year.

ACTOR   And how many people die?

ANNOUNCER   One hundred and twenty seven per minute, sixty-
              seven million a year.

LECTURER   Do the maths.

ACTOR   The world population grows by . . .

ANNOUNCER   . . . one hundred and twenty-six people a minute,
              sixty-six million a year.

LECTURER   And every one of those babies will grow up
              wanting - and some will get - new smartphones
              and the latest fashions and to fly abroad for
              holidays and a car and a home with all the latest
              gadgets.

ACTOR   So we should stop people having babies? Bring the human race to and end?

ACTOR   The planet would thank us.

ACTOR   No more oil spillages.

ACTOR   Burning of the Amazon.

ACTOR   Noisy airplanes buzzing everywhere like giant bees.

ACTOR   Animal species could revive.

ACTOR   As long as ours wasn't around.

ACTOR   Are we really ready to commit species suicide?

LECTURER   There's a compromise.

ACTOR   A compromise?

LECTURER   Ensure that everyone who wants to be a parent understands the consequences, for them and the world about them, today, tomorrow and a hundred years from now.

ACTOR   Before you become or make someone pregnant . . .

ACTOR   . . . take a test.

ACTOR   And if you pass the test . . .

ACTOR   . . . you get a licence . . .

ACTOR   . . . to procreate . . .

ACTOR   . . . up to two children in a lifetime, replacements allowed in case of early death.

ACTOR   If you get pregnant and fail the test?

ACTOR   An abortion.

ACTOR   Adoption?

ACTOR   If the adopting parents pass the test.

LECTURER	It's a reasonable request. All we ask is that every potential parent . . .
ACTOR	. . . demonstrates - *you* demonstrate you understand the consequences of your action.
ACTOR	Work out the lifetime cost of the child you want for yourself, for the state, for the planet.
ACTOR	What resources will they use? Where will they live? How will their life impact on others?
ACTOR	Which is more important - your personal desire or the needs of those around you, or the needs of your future child?
ACTOR	Don't forget the planet.
LECTURER	So, if you're a man or a woman or you don't care how you define yourself but you have sperm or an egg that you want to become human,
ACTOR	Get a licence.
ACTOR	If it's a one-night stand or a life-long relationship,
ACTOR	Get a licence.
ACTOR	If it's body to body or pipette to test-tube,
ACTOR	Get a licence.
ACTOR	If you're carrying someone else's child,
ACTOR	Get a licence.
ACTOR	If you're paying someone to have your child,
ACTOR	Get a licence.
ACTOR	If you care about the future of your child,
ACTOR	Get a licence.
ACTOR	If you commit rape . . .
ACTOR	. . . that's a whole different ballgame and you deserve your punishment . . .

ACTOR ... but if you are raped and pregnant and despite the horror and the trauma and the disgust of that event that no-one in the world but you can understand and that will last a lifetime, you should still . . .

ACTOR Get an abortion or a licence.

ACTOR That's cold.

ACTOR That's cruel.

ACTOR That's thoughtless.

ACTOR That's heartless.

ACTOR That's life.

ACTOR That's necessary.

ACTOR It's what we need for us and our descendants to survive.

ANNOUNCER IN THE YEAR TWENTY-SEVENTY THERE WILL BE TEN BILLION PEOPLE ON THIS PLANET *(diminishing)* all needing to be fed, to live in decent housing, all wanting to be educated and have work and smartphones and travel and new clothes and . . .

LECTURER We are standing on the edge of a precipice and each year hundreds and thousands and millions of people pushing us closer to the abyss. There is only one thing to do. Draw a halt to all uncontrolled conception and if you want to bring a human life into the world . . .

ALL GET A LICENCE!